MORAY COAST RAILWAYS

AUP Titles of Related Interest

SPEYSIDE RAILWAYS
Rosemary Burgess and Robert Kinghorn

HIGHLAND BRIDGES
Gillian Nelson

WATERFALLS OF SCOTLAND
Louis Stott

GRAMPIAN BATTLEFIELDS
The Historic Battles of North East Scotland from AD 84 to 1745
Peter Marren

HAMISH BROWN'S SCOTLAND
a chapbook of explorations
Hamish Brown

THE LIVING MOUNTAIN
a celebration of the Cairngorm Mountains
Nan Shepherd

POEMS OF THE SCOTTISH HILLS
an anthology selected by Hamish Brown

SPEAK TO THE HILLS
an anthology of twentieth century British and Irish mountain poetry
selected by Hamish Brown and Martyn Berry

MORAY COAST RAILWAYS

exploring the remains
and environs of
the Great North of Scotland
and Highland Railways in
Morayshire and Banffshire

Rosemary Burgess and Robert Kinghorn

ABERDEEN UNIVERSITY PRESS
Member of Maxwell Macmillan Pergamon Publishing Corporation

First published 1990
Aberdeen University Press

British Library Cataloguing in Publication Data

Burgess, Rosemary
    Moray coast railways: exploring the remains and environs
    of the Great North of Scotland and Highland Railways in
    Morayshire and Banffshire.
    1. Scotland. Grampian region — Visitors' guides
    I. Title II. Kinghorn, Robert
    914.12'104858

    ISBN 0 08 037970 2

Printed in Great Britain at
BPCC AUP-Aberdeen Ltd.
Member of BPCC Ltd.

Contents

Illustrations

Abbreviations

LOS   = Lens of Sutton
RP   = Real Photographs
JLS   = J L Stevenson
L&G   = Locomotive and General
WGD   = W G Davidson
AC   = Auchinloch Collection
CJF   = C J Fordyce
KF   = K Fenwick
AJL   = A J Lambert
ML   = Moray Libraries
PB   = Pieter Betlem
RRFK = R R F Kinghorn

Maps

All maps by James Renny

Acknowledgements

The authors would like to thank all those who have helped in the preparation of this book. This especially includes all those who have allowed us to use their copyrighted photographs, which we have gratefully and individually acknowledged below each print; The Great North of Scotland Railway Association for use of their photograph collection, the information in their Journals and that supplied by their members; those who helped provide material for the sketch maps (Keith Fenwick, Brian Wilkinson and Wilf Hodginson), as well as James Renny who redrew them; and the staff of the Imperial College Geology Photographic section who printed the photographs.

Frontispiece—GNSR class V (LNER class D40) at Banff as BR 62262 (LOS)

I

Introduction

General

This book is a companion volume to *Speyside Railways* and describes the state of the railway lines and stations along the Moray and Banff coasts and nearby, as they were and as they are now, how they came to be there, how to find what is left and what else of interest there is nearby each locality. (Map 1) Like *Speyside Railways* the title is misleading as we cover more than it indicates. However, in addition, the lines discussed in this book are mostly in the old county of Banff with only those west of the Spey in Moray. The name was chosen, however, as the GNSR coast line was always known as the Moray Firth Coast Line.

The main line described, that along the coast together with the branch to Banff, was owned by the Great North of Scotland Railway (GNSR) but the line between Keith and Portessie was a Highland Railway (HR) enterprise (Map 1). The former lines spent a quarter of the century from 1923, as part of the London & North Eastern Railway (LNER), followed by less than twenty years in the ownership of British Railways before they were closed and most of their structures demolished. The Highland branch closed before the First World War and, with the exception of a short length near Keith, was never operated by LMSR or BR.

With movable fittings such as track, signals etc removed, the buildings, embankments, bridges etc were, in general, left to their fate, although some bridges carrying the line over rivers and roads were dismantled at the time of the original closure. Luckily the great viaduct over the River Spey remains. The condition of the remainder varies greatly. Some things have totally disappeared, either by subsequent demolition of by being engulfed by nature reclaiming her own, while others are as good as new and still in use, albeit for other purposes and without tracks.

Parts of the trackbed of the lifted coast line have been opened as public paths. These include the aforementioned Spey viaduct and the

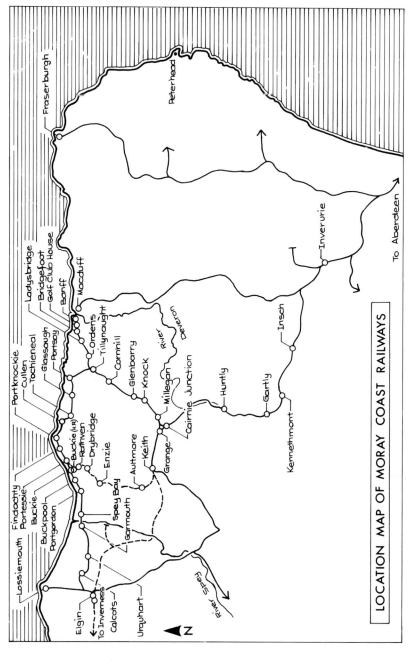

LOCATION MAP OF MORAY COAST RAILWAYS

Map 1   Location map of Moray Coast Railways

section between Portknockie and Cullen and are a very pleasant means of seeing this part of Scotland with exceptionally good views of the coast. However, this book has been written with the car driver, cyclist and road user as well as the walker in mind and, where there is a choice, the directions are given for those following the trackbed or visiting the stations by road. Where there is no alternative only the road instructions are given. The three main problems to walking the line are: construction of houses, heavy undergrowth and the removal of bridges. In general, bridges which were stone arches, both over and under, or steel girder under bridges have been left in place unless road widening has taken place. However, steel girder over bridges have in most cases been removed by the scrap merchants when the lines were dismantled.

Remember, apart from those parts converted into the public paths the remainder of the land is private and some of the surviving station buildings are houses. Always obtain permission before entering someone else's land, never damage their property or their wildlife, keep dogs under control, leave no litter and always close gates behind you.

All map references are to the metric 1 to 50,000 series Ordnance Survey maps. All distances are in miles and chains (80 chains = 1 mile), from Cairnie Junction for the ex-GNSR lines, and are based upon railway mileages.

In addition to the railway we have tried to mention some of the other things of interest or beauty which can be seen in the neighbourhood and the wild flowers now inhabiting the places where trains once ran. However, we would recommend that the facilities of the tourist boards are used as these bodies produce an excellent range of leaflets detailing all that is to be seen in each locality. They also provide a very good accommodation guide with photographs and telephone numbers which can remove many of the worries of where to spend each night.

We hope the book will be of use to those wishing to model the GNSR. Often details of rolling stock are available but the information about stations, track layouts, the sources of freight, lineside features and station impedimenta as well as the settings of the lines is more difficult to come by.

For more information about the railways in the north of Scotland, consult the histories of both the Great North of Scotland and Highland Railways, as well as albums of photographs of both, which have been published. These cover the histories, buildings, rolling stock and all the impedimenta of these lines much more fully than here. In addition there are Great North of Scotland and Highland Railway Associations which research and publish about the history of these two railways.

Outline of Railway History of the Area

The first railway proposals in North East Scotland were in 1844 for a line to link Inverness with Aberdeen, together with branches to Portsoy, Banff and Peterhead. Parliamentary powers were obtained but various financial crises delayed the construction so that on the direct route from Aberdeen to Inverness the GNSR owned only as far as Keith. Even that section was constructed and opened in two parts. The Act for GNSR from Aberdeen to Inverness with the branch to Portsoy and Banff received the Royal Assent on 26 June 1846. At that time the authorised mileage exceeded that of any other Scottish Railway. Financial difficulties meant that the Aberdeen to Huntly section was the first part built and this was formally opened on 19 September 1854. The first passenger trains ran the next day, although goods services had been operating from 12 September. On 25 May 1855 the GNSR obtained powers to extend their line to Keith, which extension was opened on Saturday, 11 October 1856.

The remainder of the route to Inverness was owned and operated by the GNSR's great rival, the Highland Railway. This had grown out of a local line (variously and chronologically the Inverness and Nairn, the Inverness and Elgin Junction and the Inverness and Aberdeen Junctions Railways) and was eventually to stretch from near Perth to Thurso and from Keith to Kyle of Lochalsh. The Inverness and Aberdeen Junction Railway opened their line to Keith on 18 August 1858.

Whilst the GNSR had been engaged in its building, other local lines had been promoted, namely the Morayshire, the Strathspey and the Banffshire Railways. The GNSR was always looking for ways to bypass the Highland and get its own access to Inverness or, at the least, increase its proportion of the mileage between the two cities of Aberdeen and Inverness. The GNSR therefore encouraged these local lines and eventually amalgamated with them. The furthest west that the GNSR ever reached was Elgin and that was by two circuitous routes. One was inland from Keith Junction via Dufftown and Craigellachie (see *Speyside Railways*) while the other, the object of part of this book, was from Cairnie Junction via the coast. (Map 1) Dates for opening and closing are given in the historical summaries at the beginning of each chapter and apply to all stations on that part of the line unless specifically mentioned in the text.

The Portsoy and Banff branches were built by an independent company, albeit with the backing of the GNSR. The Banff, Portsoy, and Strathisla Railway took over the proposed branch to Banff and

Portsoy which the GNSR had been authorised to build but had been unable to construct because of financial constraints. Later the line was operated by the GNSR, after which it was called the Banffshire Railway, and eventually the two amalgamated. Later the GNSR extended the Portsoy branch along the coast to Lossie Junction, just outside Elgin.

The lack of railway communication from the coast to Inverness and from the coast to the south caused the Highland Railway to open its branch from Keith to Portessie. This it did while the GNSR's coast line was being built.

Typical GNSR lineside features

All railways have their own styles of building and the GNSR was no exception. Because the GNSR absorbed many minor railways there are differences in architectural style between the various lines. A different selection of these several styles used by the GNSR for its more permanent structures, e.g. stations and bridges, is to be seen on this section compared with the lines covered in *Speyside Railways*. However, the smaller items such as signals and foot bridges have gone, as well as some of the more major structures.

In general, the GNSR was mainly single track with passing places, normally at stations where two platforms were provided. Only a single platform was required where there was no passing place. The two platform stations normally had the major building on the Elgin bound side, although there were exceptions. With the exception of Elgin none of the GNSR stations considered in this book were large.

The main building normally consisted of a wooden edifice, although a few were of stone construction. The wooden ones were very simple internally, containing a booking hall with ticket cum station master's office and waiting room, (see plan of Auchindachy in *Speyside Railways*). Spey Bay (1) and Urquhart (2) are typical wooden stations with conventional entrances from the road, although they are of two different variants. Spey Bay has a recessed section on the platform side whereas Urquhart is flat fronted. Cornhill (3) is typical of the wooden station types where there is no passenger entrance at the rear of the building, access presumably being via the platform. This type also has wooden extensions at each end, one of which houses the gentlemen's. A similar station building to Cornhill can be seen at Kennethmont on the still extant GNSR mainline between Keith and Aberdeen (4 and 5). Although the trains still pass here, the station is closed, so visitors to nearby Leith Hall have to travel by road. Both these are of the recessed

1   Spey Bay, recessed front station building, August 1988 (RRFK)

front variety and should be compared with the flat fronted no-access from the rear type as seen at Longmorn (*Speyside Railways*, figs 1 and 108).

Stone stations were much less common on this section, Buckie and Tillynaught being the most notable but only that at the old terminus at Portsoy survives, but these are not typical of wayside stations on this section of the GNSR.

On the opposite platforms were small wooden waiting shelters, although none along the coast section seems to have survived. Luckily on the still used mainline there are GNSR waiting shelters to be found. In the yard at Gartly station one exists (6) and at Insch there is one in situ on the platform (7).

A building important to the running of the trains is the signal box or cabin. Again none of those on the lines visited has survived. However, nearby on the mainline are two types of GNSR signal box. They were of wooden construction to match the station buildings. At Insch (8) there is a box with a toilet up the steps, but no lobby to the box and a plain hipped roof, while at Kennethmont (9) the roof is more complex and there is a small entrance lobby. (At Insch the signalman was wearing a kilt on the day we called.)

2 Urquhart, flat fronted station building, August 1988 (RRFK)

3 Cornhill, recessed front station with no rear access, August 1988 (RRFK)

4   Kennethmont Station building, August 1988 (RRFK)

5   Kennethmont, rear view, August 1988 (RRFK)

6   Gartly waiting shelter, August 1988 (RRFK)

7   Insch waiting shelter, August 1988 (RRFK)

8   Insch signal box, August 1988 (RRFK)

9   Kennethmont signal box, August 1988 (RRFK)

Where there were two platforms a footbridge was provided. The all-wooden GNSR type have all long since gone but figure 10 shows the one at Rothes on the Elgin to Craigellachie line. The LNER replaced the GNSR version, but even those have not stood the test of time and BR demolition teams. Insch, on the mainline, still boasts one of the LNER design (11). Near the site of Buckpool Station there is a different type of bridge, more reminiscent of the Highland Railway. It is of steel construction (12) with the makers plate (13) stating that it was made at the Rose Street Foundry, Inverness in 1892.

Station name boards on the GNSR were four horizontal wooden planks with a moulded surround mounted on concrete posts. The station name was in large raised letters. None on this section have survived, but name boards, albeit without the letters, can be seen at Nethybridge on the Speyside line (14) or at Keith Town.

The railway staff normally lived near the station at which they were employed and thus small houses were provided. Many on the GNSR were single storey L-shaped buildings as at Spey Bay (15). For shelter during the working day and for the storage of tools small lineside bothys or huts were provided. The GNSR sort was made of tarred sleepers and one can be seen in the yard at Maud Junction. The LNER replaced many of these with their standard concrete version, one of which is at Kennethmont (16).

10   GNSR footbridge at Rothes, looking to Craigellachie (LOS)

11   LNER footbridge at Insch, looking to Keith, August 1988 (RRFK)

12   Footbridge near Buckpool, August 1988 (RRFK)

13 Makers plate on footbridge near Buckpool, August 1988 (RRFK)

14 GNSR station sign, Nethybridge, July 1986 (RRFK)

15   GNSR station house, Spey Bay, August 1988 (RRFK)

16   LNER platelayer's hut, Kennethmont, August 1988 (RRFK)

Some of the stations had goods sheds. Probably because they were made of wood none have survived on this line in their original condition. That at Cornhill (17) is the only one but it has been covered in corrugated iron by its new owners. However, not far away one can be seen in its original condition at Inverurie, on the mainline (18). Some stations had to make do with small sleeper built platforms for the unloading of wagons, as at Kennethmont (19).

Engines needed to be watered and this was supplied from water cranes fed from water towers. None of the water cranes are extant but GNSR cranes were of similar type to Highland Railway ones, as can be seen at Buckie (20). The water towers had steel tanks on stone bases. None of the tanks have survived but some of the bases are to be seen, as at Glenbarry (21).

There is much other impedimenta to be found on GNSR stations. Station seats no longer exist on the closed stations but two types can be seen on the mainline. At Huntly a wooden seat (22) can be seen while at Insch the more fanciful cast iron and wood version is still in use (23). Weighbridges were provided at most stations. That at Huntly has its mechanism enclosed in a wooden box (24). This could be compared with the one at Aberlour (*Speyside Railways* fig 10). The GNSR normally lit its stations by oil lamps placed into brackets. Two types are to be seen, the free standing on top of a cast iron, wooden or concrete post, as at Portessie (25) or Ladysbridge (26), or those attached to buildings, e.g. at Nethybridge (*Speyside Railways* fig 12). Some early platforms were rather low and later mounting stools were provided to assist passengers. These still exist at Huntly on the mainline (27). A typical water fountain, as at Insch (28), can be seen at Spey Bay.

Mile posts with the mileage from Aberdeen in figures and dots for the quarters were placed every quarter mile but, sadly, none are to be seen on this line. Stations which had goods sidings had a loading gauge on the exit to the mainline so that nothing too large to pass by the lineside structures was allowed on to the line. The only one to be seen is at Portknockie (29). Notices not to trespass on the railway were provided wherever there was a likely place of access. The GNSR ones were all replaced by the LNER, some of whose can still be seen, e.g. at Glassaugh (30).

The railway was fenced throughout its length, often with wire between wooden posts although sometimes round cast iron ones, some marked 'Harper & Co. Abdn'. Others as used as at Portessie (31), have the inscription 'James Abernethy & Co. Aberdeen'. Although larger versions of these iron columns supported gates across roadways on other sections of the GNSR, on the coast line such gates seem to have been hung on concrete posts, as at Findochty (32). Access across the line

17   GNSR goods shed, Cornhill, August 1988 (RRFK)

18   GNSR goods shed, Inverurie, August 1988 (RRFK)

19 Sleeper built goods dock, Kennethmont, August 1988 (RRFK)

20 GNSR water crane, Buckie, looking to Elgin (L&G)

21   Base of GNSR water tower, Glenbarry, August 1988 (RRFK)

22   Wooden seat, Huntly, August 1988 (RRFK)

23 Cast iron and wood seat, Insch, August 1988 (RRFK)

24 Weighbridge, Huntly, August 1988 (RRFK)

25   GNSR lamp bracket, Portessie, August 1988 (RRFK)

26   GNSR lamp bracket, Ladysbridge, looking to Banff, August 1988 (RRFK)

27   Passenger mounting stool, Huntly, August 1988 (RRFK)

28   Passenger drinking fountain, Insch, August 1988 (RRFK)

29   Loading gauge, Portknockie, looking east, August 1988 (RRFK)

30   LNER trespass notice, Glassaugh, August 1988 (RRFK)

31   GNSR fencing post, marked James Abernethy & Co, Aberdeen at
            Portessie, August 1988 (RRFK)

32   Concrete gate posts, Findochty, August 1988 (RRFK)

for pedestrians was by kissing gates (*Speyside Railways* fig 15), but none can be seen on the coast line today. Fencing around station houses on the sections was with wooden fencing, as at Tochieneal (33).

The railway used a variety of bridges to cross and be crossed. The most famous on the whole coast line must be that which crosses the Spey at Spey Bay. When built its 350 foot central bow string girder span was over the river and the approach viaducts consisting of six shorter 100 foot girder spans were over the flood plain of the river. A couple of years after its construction the river changed course and ever since has flowed under part of the eastern approach viaduct (34). Masonry viaducts are also a famous feature of this line, the most notable being at Cullen (35) but smaller ones are to be seen, e.g. near Buckpool (36, map reference 405646, OS sheet 28, Elgin). Smaller over bridges sometimes had curved abutments, as at Porttannachy (37) or straight ones as at Millegan (38). On other occasions, as west of Buckie (map reference 425657, OS sheet 28, Elgin, 39), the road crossed on a bridge with steel girders and steel sidesheets on brick pillars. On a similar bridge at Knock the sidesheets have a cast motif which consists of a buckled belt in an oval. In the top section of the belt is 'James Abernethy & Co.' with the words 'Engineers' and 'Ironmongers' to the left and right of the buckle respectively. In the centre of the belt is the date 1898, with 'Ferryhill Foundary' on top and 'Aberdeen' below.

33   GNSR fencing, Tochieneal, August 1988 (RRFK)

34   GNSR Spey Viaduct, eastern approach, August 1988 (RRFK)

35   GNSR Cullen Viaduct, looking west, August 1988 (RRFK)

36   GNSR viaduct near Buckpool, August 1988 (RRFK)

37   GNSR overbridge near Porttannachy, August 1988 (RRFK)

38 GNSR overbridge at Millegan, August 1988 (RRFK)

39 GNSR overbridge at Buckie, August 1988 (RRFK)

Elgin was the only station to have elaborate glass canopies over the platforms (40), although those over the terminus platforms at the east of the station have been removed.

40   GNSR glass canopies, Elgin (L&G)

Typical HR lineside features

Having been closed so long ago there is much less evidence of the Highland's permanent structures. However, the station buildings were of wooden construction (140), although none are still extant on this line. The nearest wooden HR station building to here is that at Burghead (*Speyside Railways*, fig 126). Two different designs of HR stone built houses for the station staff can be seen at Rathven (139) and Enzie (133 and 134). At Aultmore station there are the remains of HR gates (41). At Portessie are the remains of the Highland water tower and turntable.

For other information about HR lineside features consult any of the books about the Highland Railway.

41   HR gates, Aultmore, August 1988 (RRFK)

Landscape, Flora and Fauna

Exploring disused railways is an excellent way to observe relatively undisturbed wildlife and plants, and the area encompassed by this book should provide a rich variety of both flora and fauna. Please remember to respect the Country Code—do not disturb wildlife and never pick or uproot the plants.

   Geologically the area of North East Scotland is principally a worn-down platform of resistant and very ancient metamorphic rocks, mostly Dalradian. This has been blanketed by boulder clays and gravels from successive Ice Ages, producing rolling countryside, and notable terminal moraines of coarse gravels near the mouth of the Spey—especially between Fochabers and Lhanbryde. Quartz-rich bands among the highly folded rocks between Cullen and Portsoy produce spectacular cliffs. To the west of Buckie, along a strip parallel with the coast, is the Old Red Sandstone. There is also an outcrop of Old Red Sandstone inland from Cullen. A band of metamorphosed rocks runs north to meet the coast near Portsoy. The Serpentine, which is produced there, is a weathering product of the Olivine found in igneous rocks or metamorphosed limestones.

The railways described pass through mixed farmland and woodland, as well as along the Moray coast, alternatively cliffs and low dunes, and across the spectacular Spey estuary. Inland we will encounter other river valleys such as that of the Isla and the Deveron, and pleasant rolling countryside rising to 1,409 feet at Knock Hill—a surprising name as Knock already means 'hill' in Gaelic! The Moray coast is famous for its mild 'riviera' climate, and in the section we explore, from the mouth of the Spey to Banff, we find many varieties of interesting plants. The scenery too is very attractive, and the beaches, harbours and cliffs are well worth exploring. Look out specially for the Bow Fiddle Rock at Portknockie, an arched stack formed of Cullen quartzite, and the Three Kings at Cullen, fine stacks of Old Red Sandstone, found on a raised beach.

There are some special features about the habitat near old railway lines as opposed to the countryside in general. Firstly, there are plants which have grown directly as a result of the railway's presence, such as rosebay willow herb, found in nearly every location. This very successful 'weed' first became well known after the Second World War when it was known as fireweed because it was usually found on land that had been bombed and burnt. This is no coincidence as the plant actually thrives on the extra nitrates in the soil produced by burning. Thus it took readily to railway embankments, which were quite often burnt, either accidentally, in the days of steam, or deliberately as a measure to control vegetation. The airborn seeds were also carried along by the trains, so this plant has truly taken advantage of the railways. Secondly, the habitat is unusual as, except where the railway track has been completely ploughed out, it is normally untouched by agriculture, and being relatively undisturbed, some rare species of wildlife can thrive. In fact, some vegetation thrives so well as to completely block the trackbed, especially in cuttings! Gorse, broom and sapling trees are the culprits here. A third special feature which will be observed is that around the station sites there were once cultivated gardens, and the feral descendents of lupins, sweet peas, honeysuckle and roses can be found. If one explores further in the station master's garden or cottage gardens, one will also find gooseberries, raspberries, blackberries and mint.

Coastal Section

Accompanied by the scream of seagulls, one can find many varieties of seaside plants which are tolerant of a salty environment. On the sand dunes such as to the west of Cullen and of Banff are many hardy grasses, and the cliffs overlooking the Bow Fiddle Rock are covered with yellow toadflax in summer. From many of the coastal station sites, excellent views of the coast can be obtained, and around you are scabious, gorse, yarrow, eyebrite, celadine and many, many others. At the mouth of the Spey is a deltaic area which supports many colonies of birds including grey wagtails, common terns, mergansers, goosanders and black headed gulls. Bring your binoculars to spot the wide variety of seabirds and grey seals on this part of the coast.

Inland Lines

For much of their routes these railways pass through arable farmland where crops such as oats, turnips, barley, clover and grass may be seen, with sheep and cattle. Rotation of crops is usually practised so there is little permanent grassland. Watch out for rabbits, moles, hedgehogs, shrews, stoats and others—not all welcome to farmers! In summer the quiet deserted stations are full of small birds, animals and butterflies. There are also areas of both deciduous and coniferous plantations.

Scotch Whisky

Whisky is an anglicisation of the gaelic 'uisge beatha' meaning water of life. The basic definition of whisky is incorporated in law, normally the Finance Act, because of the duty paid on it. Forthcoming EEC legislation will define all European spirits in terms of their alcohol content. The term 'Scotch' means that it has been distilled and matured in Scotland. Likewise Irish Whiskey has been distilled and matured in Ireland. Bourbon Whiskey is made from a mash of not less than 51 per cent corn grain and must be produced in the USA whereas Rye Whiskey must be produced from a mash of not less than 51 per cent rye grain.

The oldest reference to whisky in Scotland is in the Scottish Exchequer Rolls for 1494. In 1644 the Scots Parliament passed an Excise Act fixing the duty at 2s. 8d. per pint. The Scottish and English Crowns were united in 1603 and in 1707 the Act of Union united the Parliaments. However, that Act did not abolish the frontier as far as 'Colonial Liquors', which included Scotch Whisky, were concerned. Thus when the North British Railway started to run trains into England in 1846 there were delays as the customs men searched the luggage. Until the law was changed the NBR posted notices warning travellers not to take whisky into England.

Malt whisky is made from malted barley in a traditional pot still whereas grain whisky is produced from a mixture of malted barley and unmalted cereals in a patent or continuous still. Although many single malt whiskies are sold, the bulk of whiskies are blended mixtures of up to fifty individual whiskies. Both malt and grain whiskies are left to mature in casks made of oak, often old sherry casks. The law says that this shall be for at least three years but many malts are left for fifteen to twenty-one years. After maturation and blending the whisky is reduced to the required strength by the addition of soft water.

A comparison of a location map of whisky distilleries and the railways of North East Scotland would show a marked correlation. That is no coincidence as most of the distilleries in the area came after the railway. The rivers provided the water of the required quality while the railway provided the transport for the inward coal and grain and the outward whisky.

However, although there are fewer distilleries in the vicinity of the railways covered by this book than by *Speyside Railways,* there are some, e.g. at Glassaugh and Knock. For a description of the production of whisky and its intimate relationships with the railways of North East Scotland see *Speyside Railways.*

II

Cairnie Junction to Banff

History of the section

From the earliest interests in railways in this part of Scotland it was realised that there was a need for railway communication with the Banff coast. The problem was the hills of Knock and Aultmore between Keith and the sea. The original Act which authorised the construction of the GNSR mainline from Aberdeen towards Inverness contained powers for a branch to Portsoy and Banff, both of which were thriving harbours. This was to run through the gap of Glenbarry, east of Aultmore.

However, the financial crash, which delayed the construction of the main line, meant that the GNSR would not be able to build the branch for some considerable time. Thus on 27 July 1857 the Banff, Portsoy and Strathisla Railway was authorised to build a $16\frac{1}{4}$ mile line from Grange to Banff Harbour and a $3\frac{1}{4}$ mile branch from Tillynaught to Portsoy (Map 2). The branches were opened on 30 July 1859 but a derailment prevented full services until 2 August. As from 1 February 1863 the GNSR worked the line for 60 per cent of the receipts. An Act of 21 July 1863 confirmed this and authorised a $14\frac{1}{4}$ mile extension from Portsoy to Port Gordon. At this time the name was changed to the Banffshire Railway. The Banff line was treated as the main line until the opening of the coast line, after which it became the branch.

The Act of 30 July 1866 allowed the GNSR to amalgamate with its various subsidiaries but the financial position of the Banffshire Railway precluded this. However, a year later the amalgamation took place and was confirmed by the Act of 12 August 1867, which also allowed for the abandonment of the Port Gordon extension.

To keep the costs as low as possible the line involved severe gradients such as the four miles from Grange to Glenbarry at about 1 in 100, or the 1 in 70 $3\frac{1}{2}$ mile section from Cornhill to Glenbarry and the final 2 miles into Portsoy.

All the stations on the Banff branch closed on 6 July 1964 for

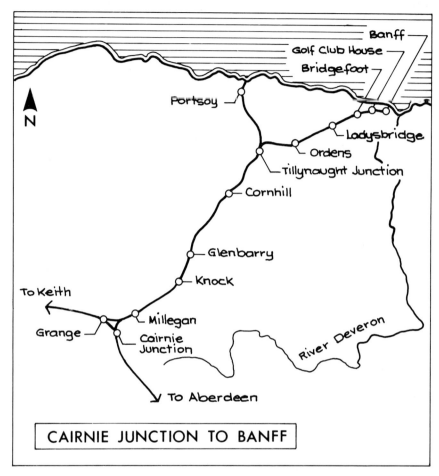

Map 2   Cairnie Junction to Banff via Tillynaught (GNSR)

passengers but the line together with Ladysbridge and Banff were open for freight until 6 May 1968, when the whole of the coast line was closed.

Early services comprised three trains a day each way between Grange and Banff. Of these, two were mixed goods and passenger. Portsoy was served by a branch service from Tillynaught three times a day, two of which carried goods as well and one service from Banff to Portsoy. Journey times varied between an hour and $1\frac{1}{4}$ hours. By the 1880s the line was open to Tochieneal and the services were changing with five services per day between Grange and Tochieneal. By now the Banff line was the branch on which there were six trains each way per day. Grange to Tochieneal took about an hour while Banff to Tillynaught required

10 to 15 minutes. By 1902 the pattern of services had settled down and was to remain very little altered until closure. Usually there were three trains from Aberdeen along the coast line per day and three others from Keith giving connections to and from Aberdeen. The time from Elgin to Aberdeen was about $2\frac{3}{4}$ to 3 hours and this had been changed little by 1951.

Grange (496506 OS sheet 29, Banff)

The site of Grange station is best approached by turning south off the A95 at 488513 just after this road crosses the river, turn sharp left to the station site. A gravel drive leads to a small house and overgrown track sides.

Grange was the original junction for the line to Portsoy and Banff and, situated on the Aberdeen side, had a single storey stone H-shaped building with a wood and glass partition between the arms of the 'H' on the platform side (42). Sadly almost all evidence of it has disappeared. All that is to be seen is the Inverness bound platform, a small gate (43), the possible base of a building on the Aberdeen side, two LNER trespass notices, one GNSR fence post and what was probably a railwayman's house.

When leaving the station site do not turn left, back across the River Isla, but follow the road alongside the river. After a mile the site of a level crossing at the junction of the two loops to the main line is found (506505).

Cairnie Junction (504497, OS sheet 29, Banff)

Continue along this road and the site of the station with the outlines of the island platform can be seen from the bridge over the main line (44 and 45). The station consisted of a wooden building with steel and glass canopies situated on the island platform, together with assorted sidings (Map 3). There is no access to the site of the station as it is BR property with the single remaining track still in use. There appears to be much vegetation alongside the track with some newly planted fir trees, as well as banks of rosebay willow herb, broom, thistles and ragwort. Against the wall of the farmhouse just across the bridge is the 30 mph speed restriction sign for the old coast line junction. Return to the site of the north junction. The mainline and the coast line branch are double track but the line from Grange, completing the triangle, was single. The coast line became single immediately before the Grange North Junction which was a simple divergence of a single track into two.

42   Grange Station, looking to Cairnie Junction, August 1988 (RRFK)

43   Grange Station, Looking to Cairnie Junction (L&G)

44 Cairnie Junction, looking to Keith, 2 October 1954 (JLS)

45 Cairnie Junction looking to Keith, August 1988 (RRFK)

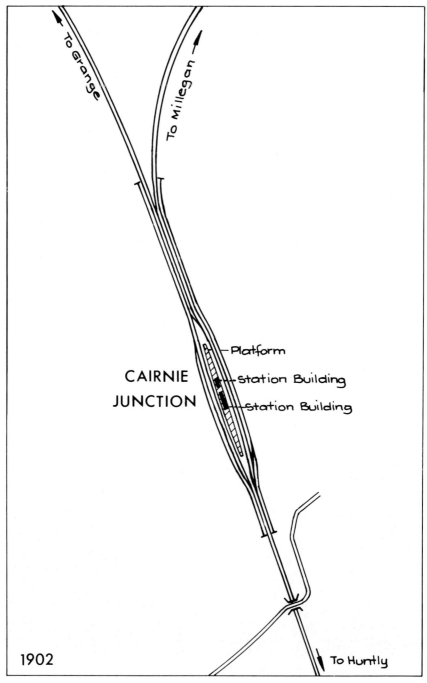

To Grange

To Millegan

Platform

Station Building

Station Building

CAIRNIE
JUNCTION

1902

To Huntly

Map 3   Cairnie Junction

Grange North Junction 38c (506505, OS sheet 29, Banff)

From this point it is possible to walk some of the way towards Cairnie Junction along the old trackbed. From here northwards the trackbed can be driven along at least as far as the site of Millegan Station, giving a good view of the River Isla from the old bridge, and may be walked further than that (46). Just north of the junction one crosses from Aberdeenshire into Banffshire.

If not wishing to drive or walk along the line, return to the A95 and turn right, to the east.

Millegan 1m 20c (516509, OS sheet 29, Banff)

At the B9117 (507513) turn right to the site of Millegan Station.

The station has been completely destroyed and we can find no record of what type it was. The only indication of anything ever having been there is the wide drive in from the road. If you have driven on the trackbed from Grange Junction it is best to re-join the road here.

In the early timetables this station was also spelt Millagan. Whether it was late in building or an afterthought is not known but it did not

46   Millegan, looking north (AC)

open until 1 October 1859. If a second thought it would seem that the first thought had been correct as it closed for passengers in October 1865 and completely by either 1 July or 1 October 1875.

Either walk along the trackbed towards Knock or turn left along the B9117. To the west can be seen Shiel and Knock woods with Knock Hill rising up to the north west. Agriculture in this area is mostly mixed arable and cattle. Be careful not to leave any gates open. On this section of the trackbed, which is like a broad, gravel farm track, look out for massive sleeper fencing and some GNSR gateposts and gates made by 'Blaikie of Abdn.'

This walk through farmland provides an opportunity to look out for the many birds of this area. One of the commonest is rooks, the density having been recorded as one bird per 3 acres. One can also see corn buntings, skylarks, meadow pipits and curlews which, together with oystercatchers, favour arable land for nest sites. Herring gulls, however, only venture inland to feed and prefer to nest in cliff colonies.

Knock 3m 40c (546530, OS sheet 29, Banff)

Continue along the B9177 to the B9022 and turn left. At 551524 turn left on an unclassified road towards Knock.

The station is just north of the disused Knockdhu Distillery of James Munro and Son Ltd on the right of the road, which still crosses the trackbed by the old bridge with the oval buckle shaped scroll on its side sheets (47 and 48). GNSR gates are at the station entrance. The site is open and clear of undergrowth, the platform and trackbed being covered by short grass.

The wooden station building was of the smaller variety with the glass frontage to the platform. As late as 1927 there were two platforms and a passing loop (Map 4).

Sadly the building has been destroyed, but its base on the remains of the up platform can be easily identified along with the two posts which supported the main nameboard. Behind these can still be seen the sleeper-built containers observable in the old photograph. At the northern end of the platform is a GNSR lampholder. The loading bay behind the platform can still be discerned. There is a raised roadway leading up to it, a deep stone wall on the distillery side, a shallow stone wall to the platform and the steps at the north east corner. The down platform has disappeared completely (49 and 50).

To the north west of the track is Knock Hill, which rises to 1,409 feet. It is probably a tautological name as Cnoc (pronounced knock) in Gaelic means hill. Many places have such tautological names, possibly

47 Knock Station, looking north, 7 October 1954 (JLS)

48 Knock Station, looking north, August 1988 (RRFK)

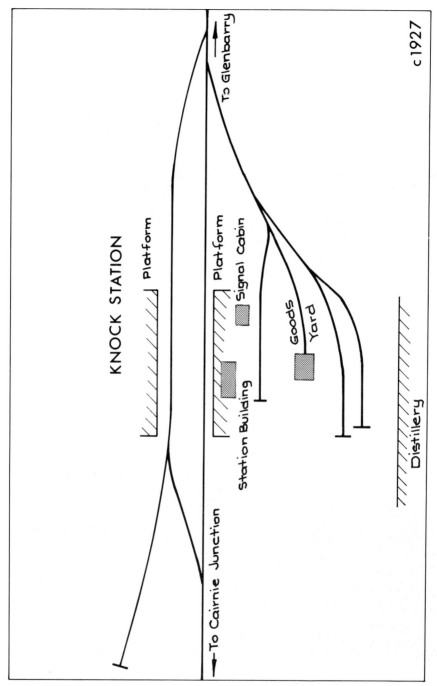

KNOCK STATION

c 1927

Platform

Platform

Signal Cabin

Station Building

Goods Yard

To Glenbarry

To Cairnie Junction

Distillery

Map 4   Knock

49   Knock Station, looking to Keith, 7 October 1954 (JLS)

50   Knock Station, looking to Keith, August 1988 (RRFK)

due to incomers who did not speak the native language asking what a place was, meaning its place-name and were told its topographic description, to which they added their own topographic name; hence Knock Hill or Hill Hill!

Either, continue walking to Glenbarry or, return to the B road and turn left onto the A95.

Glenbarry 4m 64c (555548, OS sheet 29, Banff)

Just after joining the A95, park in lay-by on the right opposite garage. The site of Glenbarry Station is along the track by the side of the garage and is the garage's property.

Glenbarry had two platforms and a footbridge. On the Grange bound side was the main single storey building and a signal box, while the other platform boasted a typical little GNSR waiting shelter and larger stone building (Map 5).

The site of the station is fiercely overgrown and covered with scrap vehicles. The most prominent remain is the stone building on the Elgin platform (51) which can be identified in the old photograph (52). The edges of the platform are just visible and the cut off bases of the rail-built LNER type footbridge can be seen amidst the dense undergrowth: broom, rosebay willow herb and small trees. The wooden sleeper decking at the level crossing and some other sleepers with various metal fittings can be seen to the north of the station.

This station did not open until 1 October 1859 but survived to close at the same time as all the others.

From here northwards the line is much more overgrown than to the south, however it is probably passable to the more intrepid. Alternatively, proceed along the A95. The stream which runs along the line from here to Tillynaught is the Burn of Boyne.

Cornhill 7m 52c (581589, OS sheet 29, Banff)

In the village of Cornhill turn left on to the B9023 at 584582.

Here we have a pleasant surprise. As one leaves the main road one catches a glimpse amongst the trees of the station which, unexpectedly, has survived.

The best entry to the station is just after the Aberdeen and Northern Marts Ltd and is marked by a GNSR gate with one GNSR post.

The station was a simple affair consisting of one platform on the west of the track with a recessed front GNSR wooden building, together with a siding which served a goods shed (53, Map 6).

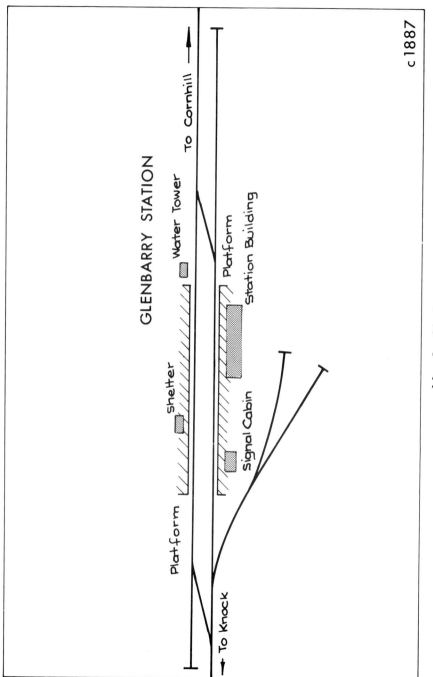

Map 5   Glenbarry

51   Glenbarry, looking north, August 1988 (RRFK)

52   Glenbarry, looking north, 7 October 1954 (JLS)

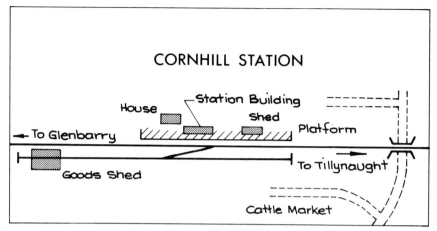

Map 6   Cornhill

The station site and building are rented from BR by a coal merchant who has erected black corrugated iron fencing around the north eastern end of the site. The station building is of the recessed front GNSR wooden type and, sitting on its platform, is extant although a bit shabby with its windows covered in corrugated iron (3 and 54). The trackbed and platform are covered with loose and bagged coal and the impedimenta associated with that trade.

To the south of the station is the loading dock and GNSR goods shed which has been covered in more of the ubiquitous corrugated iron. However, in this case it is smartly painted and the shed seems to function as the merchant's office.

Behind the station can be seen the station master's house. This is now a private residence and there is no access to it from the station. By leaving the station yard and turning left one may walk past the site of the demolished overbridge, after which on the left is the drive to the house. Good views of the rear of the station building (55) can be obtained and it will be observed that there was no passenger entry to the station building from this side.

One might find small animals such as bank voles, shrews and stoats in this location, but there are very few badgers or foxes in the north east of Scotland.

Cornhill is a faming village which still has a weekly livestock mart every Thursday. There is an annual race to the top of nearby Knock Hill each June and the August Flower Show is another highlight of the village's life. To the west is the village of Deskford which has an interesting old church.

53   Cornhill, looking north, May 1968 (KF)

54   Cornhill, August 1988 (RRFK)

55   Cornhill from the rear, August 1988 (RRFK)

The walking around Cornhill is very easy. The roads provide varied walking through woodland and Knock Hill, 3 miles south west of the village, gives superb views over the countryside with views both across the Moray Firth to Caithness and to the Cairngorms. It has heather clad sides and can be climbed from any side but that from Glenbarry is the most popular. The southwest slope is covered with burial mounds, believed to mark graves from a battle against the Danes.

Continue on the B9023 pass the station and turn right onto the B9022.

Tillynaught 10m 11c (601618, OS sheet 29, Banff)

At Nether Dykehead (578622) turn right on to an unclassified road at the telephone box. Follow this road and turn right at 597618. The entry to the station is marked by a GNSR gate.

When the Banff, Portsoy and Strathisla Railway first opened, Tillynaught was a simple junction (Map 7). It consisted of a Vee shaped island platform with one siding, entered from the south, alongside the Banff line.

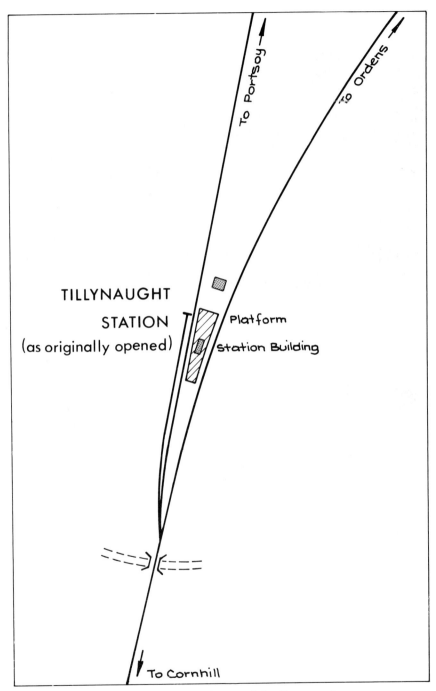

Map 7   Tillynaught as originally opened

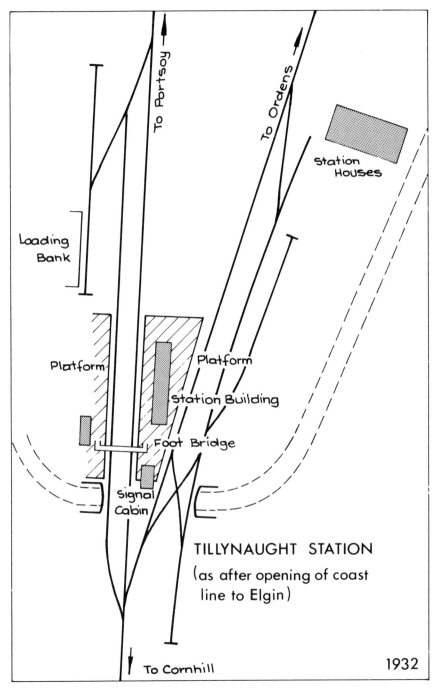

To Portsoy →

To Ordens →

Station Houses

Loading Bank

Platform

Platform

Station Building

Foot Bridge

Signal Cabin

TILLYNAUGHT STATION

(as after opening of coast line to Elgin)

↓ To Cornhill

1932

Map 8   Tillynaught after opening of coast line

When the coast line opened, a side platform on the west, which was approached from the road, was added together with more sidings (Map 8). This new platform was connected to the island platform by a footbridge. This was originally a GNSR one but later renewed with LNER type. A signal box stood at the south end of the island platform by the bridge over the road to the station houses (56 and 57) On the platform by the road was a small waiting shelter, while on the island platform was a larger wooden building with an all round steel and glass canopy which was later removed (58).

The whole station site is heavily overgrown all buildings demolished and the trackbed has been filled in up to platform level. Immediately inside the gate can be seen some rail and a GNSR lampholder. The beds of the two routes can be identified in the distance as the embankments sweep away to the north.

To the south of the station site is the large underbridge, at least 20 yards wide, which used to span the width of the station, but crosses only a narrow lane. The steel girders have been removed but the massive stone retaining walls are still extant. From the top of these can be seen one of the platform ramps and the edges of some of the platforms can also be discerned, albeit with some difficulty (59). Passing through the bridge abutments and following the track one comes to the abandoned station houses. A row of terraced dwellings whose gardens are rapidly returning to the wild. Even two or three years ago these gardens were full of fruit bushes, iris and lupin, but they now seem to have been ploughed and have become agricultural land. The houses give a rather eerie sensation, dark against the sky and the wind making the doors creak on their long unoiled hinges.

Tillynaught Junction did not open until a month after the line, on 1 September 1859. Originally trains split here with parts going to Banff and Portsoy.

Return to the telephone box (597618) and turn right. At the A98 turn right.

Ordens 11m 67c (622631, OS sheet 29, Banff)

Continue along the A98 until where, shortly after the A95 from Cornhill joins from the right, an unclassified road crosses the main road. Turn right along this road, signposted Hilton 1½ miles, coming away from the trees and into wide wheat fields. The station is on the right of the bridge over the trackbed but because it is a narrow road with passing places one cannot park until some distance further on. Walk back to the bridge.

56   Tillynaught, looking north (L&G)

57   Tillynaught, looking north, August 1988 (RRFK)

58   Tillynaught, looking north (RP)

59   Tillynaught, looking north, August 1988 (RRFK)

60   Ordens, looking to Tillynaught, 4 October 1954 (JLS)

61   Ordens, looking to Tillynaught, August 1988 (RRFK)

Again we have a surprise. This station (60) was a small halt, not even advertised as a public station between October 1863 and 14 July 1924, which possessed as its sole building a small timber hut. In spite of its construction and small size one can see from the bridge that it still exists (61), together with some wooden platform edging. The road bridge has steel girders on stone abutments with fencing sides. The remains of the sleeper fencing by the trackside and some GNSR fence posts marked 'Blaikie of Abd' are to be seen. All traces of the siding opposite the platform (Map 9) have gone.

The trackbed at this locality is fairly overgrown, although probably not impassable to those prepared to deal with brambles and gorse. Others may wish to return to the A98 and turn right. Opposite the road to Boyndie on the left is a small turning to Mill of Blairshinnock. Just beyond two small bridges over the Burn of Boyndie is the remains of Blairshinnock level crossing—four massive concrete gate posts and two smaller posts for trespass signs (62 and 63).

Ladysbridge 13m 66c (651636, OS sheet 29, Banff)

Continue along the A98 and turn right onto the B9121, signposted to Turriff. Cross the stream and the station is immediately on the right with a 15 foot railway gate to the yard, level crossing gates, posts and a wicket gate.

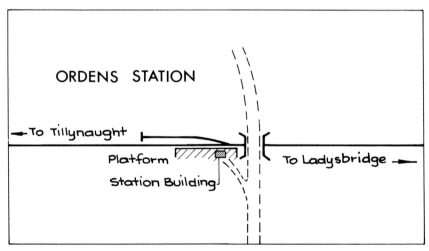

Map 9   Ordens

62 Blairshinnock Crossing, looking north, 4 October 1954 (JLS)

63 Blairshinnock Crossing, looking north, August 1988 (RRFK)

This little wayside station possessed but a single platform and typical GNSR smaller flat fronted wooden station building facing east (64 and 26). Opposite this was a goods loading bay and a goods yard (Map 10).

The site is very overgrown and all the buildings have been demolished. It is impossible to walk along the trackbed or to gain access to the platform due to the luxuriant vegetation, both trackbed and platform being deep with grasses, fireweed, yarrow, knapweed, ragwort, brambles, ox-eye daisies . . . and many more. However, the edge of the platform and a lampholder on it can be seen. A walk along the goods yard or the loading bay platform is rewarded with a GNSR lampholder and the base of a crane (26). By the entrance can be seen the wooden buffer stop (65) which ended the track alongside the loading bay (66) and the base of a platelayers hut.

From here the trackbed could be walkable to the more adventurous but in places, e.g. where the road crosses it at 659641, it has been obliterated. Return to the A98 and turn right.

64   Ladysbridge, looking to Banff, 4 October 1954 (JLS)

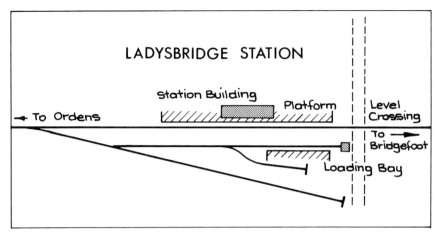

Map 10   Ladysbridge

Boyndie 15m 02c (668643, OS sheet 29, Banff)

Here there was a private siding serving the Inverboyndie distillery which was open by 1885. The distillery was bombed by the Germans during the war. The next morning three neighbouring pigs must have had monumental porcine hangovers as they were among the first on the scene of devastation and happily got the worse for the drink as they lapped up the whisky spilling from the vats! No doubt the Customs and Excise were not amused, however they could do little about it, but the bacon from those three must have had a good flavour! The distillery is being demolished at the moment (August 1988) and there seems to be no sign of the siding, although from the road a viaduct at the back of the distillery crossing the Burn of Boyndie can be seen.

Bridgefoot 15m 09c (670644, OS sheet 29, Banff)

Turn left off the A98 towards the Links Hotel. At the sharp corner just before the hotel the bridge has been removed and the road widened. Turn left and continue to a field gate before parking.
    The station was a sleeper built platform with a wooden shed (67) situated on top of the bank at this point. The locals pronounced it 'Brigfit'. Originally it was a private halt for the house, which is now the hotel, built for Lord Dawson of Penn, the Royal physician who signed

65   Ladysbridge, looking to Banff (L&G)

66   Ladysbridge, August 1988 (RRFK)

67   Bridgefoot, looking to Banff, 4 October 1954 (JLS)

68   Bridgefoot, looking to Banff, August 1988 (RRFK)

69   Banff Bay showing hotel and Bridgefoot halt, 1949 (PB)

King George V's death certificate. Many trains were not scheduled to call here and passengers intending to alight here had to ask the driver at Tillynaught to stop (see endpiece). The station has all been removed but its site and the trackside fence at that point can still be seen (68), although the site is now situated in a lush meadow of long grasses interspersed with harebells and ladies-slipper. The doctor's house, all that is left of the station and the magnificent sweep of the bay can be seen in fig 69.

Return to the A98 and turn left or cross the road at the site of the bridge, climb the concrete steps and walk along the track all the way to Banff.

Golf Club House 15m 432c (677646, OS sheet 29, Banff)

Stop in the layby at 678644. From here a path leads down the cliff to the station site, passing between the abutments of a small overbridge, no 465.

This halt was originally open all year but by 1920 it was closed between December and April. By 1960 it was only open between May and September. It had a wooden platform like Bridgefoot but did not possess the little hut as a shelter (70). Now nothing remains except for the bridge abutments and the barrel topped concrete hut (71).

Either continue along the A98 or walk along the trackbed to Banff. This is at the foot of the cliffs, beside the golf links and the sea and is a very pleasant walk, even for those normally exploring in cars. The grassy dunes and cliffs give wonderful views of the coast, and quantities of tortoiseshell butterflies can be found in summer.

Banff 16m 21c (688647, OS sheet 29, Banff)

The trackbed leads directly to the station site. Following the road takes one into Banff, an ancient small town situated at the mouth of the River Deveron. Turn left at the A97, just past the excellent little baker, and head towards the harbour, turning left at the sea.

Here we have great disappointment. Almost everything has been destroyed to put a new road along the edge of the coast. Like many GNSR branch terminii, e.g. Portsoy or Macduff, the station consisted of a goods shed and a fine trainshed (frontispiece and 72) which have now both gone but their location can be identified by the rock formation with the quartz vein in the cliff behind the site (73). Likewise the engine shed (74), which had an iron water tank on a stone base at its southern

70   Golf Clubhouse, looking to Banff, 4 October 1954 (JLS)

71   Golf Clubhouse, looking to Banff, August 1988 (RRFK)

72 Banff Station (L&G)

73 Site of Banff Station, August 1988 (RRFK)

end, has vanished but again its site is locatable by the fencing on the hill top (75). Past the station ran a line on to the harbour (Map 11).

Sadly, even the little narrow gauge railway, which for a few years ran from the site of the station to the holiday camp, has now gone.

The grass area above the station site is called 'Battery Green' and to the west of that was a place called 'Rope Walk', doubtless where the ships ropes were twisted.

The Royal and Ancient Burgh of Banff, situated where the River Deveron meets the Moray Firth, dates back to 1120. It was a frequent port of call for ships sailing between the Mediterranean and the Baltic and thus became one of the towns in the Hanseatic league, a trading alliance of the twelfth century. It was granted a charter in 1163 by Malcolm IV and in 1324 Robert the Bruce granted the town further privileges. Its first harbour was built in 1175 and this was expanded to meet the needs of the growing herring fishing industry which once had over 90 boats and dispatched 30,000 barrels a year in the 1830s. Now the remainder of the fishing has moved elsewhere and Banff harbour is used by leisure sailors.

Because of its attractive location, the gentry of the seventeenth and eighteenth centuries favoured Banff and left a legacy of fine buildings and town houses, which form the basis of a conservation area. Many of the finest buildings are identified by plaques and a booklet on them is available from the tourist office. Banff Museum, in the High Street, houses other artifacts of Banff's history. In the Low Street is the Mercat Cross, a sixteenth century carved crucifix, and next to it is a cannon captured at Sevastopol in 1855. Here was the site of the town gallows where James MacPherson was hanged. Nearby was a clock, now removed to the castellated clocktower, erected in 1839, in the midst of the crossroads in the centre of Dufftown. It was known as the 'hanging clock', or 'the clock that hanged MacPherson', because an Earl of Fife, Lord Braco, had advanced the clock so that the execution of MacPherson of Kingussie, (a freebooter who was popular with the people but not with his lordship) occurred before the reprieve reached Banff. MacPherson's last request was for a fiddle on which he played a tune, later known as 'MacPherson's Rant', to which Robert Burns was to add words.

Banff as a holiday centre has three things in its favour. Firstly it is the administrative capital of the area and thus has a fine range of facilities, shops, eating places, banks and entertainments. It is situated with beautiful coasts, both sandy beaches and spectacular cliffs, to east and west and lovely countryside to the south. Lastly it is very mild and one of the sunniest and driest towns in Scotland. To augment its natural advantages, the authorities have provided a range of leisure and

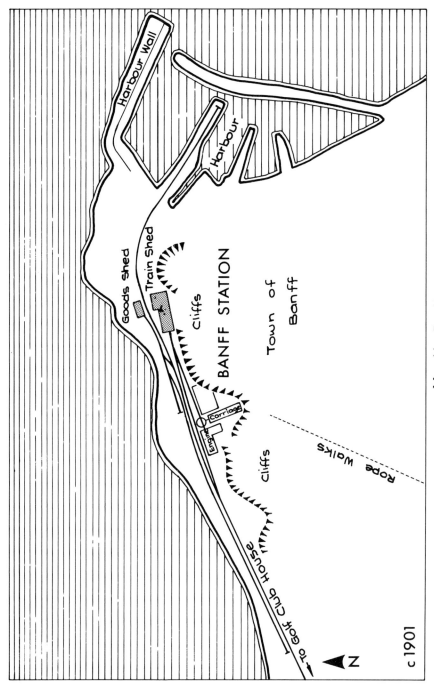

Map 11 Banff

74   Banff engine shed (L&G)

75   Site of Banff engine shed, August 1988 (RRFK)

sporting activities, including golf, swimming (both sea and pool), watersports, fishing, bowling and tennis. Caravan and camping sites are situated on Banff and Boyndie bays.

Banff Castle is an Adam mansion, built in 1750 for Lord Deskford, on the site of a medieval fortress. However, part of the original earthworks and 144 foot long curtain walls are preserved. In the grounds is an Aracaris tree which was planted in honour of General José San Martin who spent part of his exile in Banff. In recognition of this there is a Plaza Banff in Buenos Aires.

Duff House is to the south of the town by the river Deveron. Like the castle it is also to the design of William Adam, but in this case modelled on the Villa Borghese. However, because of disputes between him and the owner, Lord Braco (later Earl of Fife) it was never completed or lived in by its originator. Only the central portion, which cost £70,000 and was meant to contain the public rooms, was built with the wings for the bedrooms and service rooms uncompleted. Thus it was almost impossible to use as a dwelling and has been an hotel, prisoner of war camp and a hospital. It is now being slowly restored by the Department of the Environment. It is situated in wooded grounds which run along the river. There is a 2 mile walk through the grounds, past the Duff mausoleum and the ice house, to the Bridge of Alvah. This is a single arch built high across a spectacular gorge of the Deveron in 1772.

Banff Bridge is a seven arched bridge across the Deveron, built by Smeaton in 1779. It carries the main road to Macduff, the neighbouring town on the other side of the estuary. Until 1783 this was a hamlet called Doune, but it was then made a burgh of barony for the second Earl of Fife and it grew rapidly thereafter. Large flocks of gulls congregate at the mouth of the Deveron and in the early part of the year can include glaucous, or Icelandic gulls, blown down from the Arctic. There are also the commoner guillemots, herring gulls, fulmars, gannets and perhaps goldeneye, eider and red-breasted mengansers.

East of Macduff are the picturesque fishing villages of Gardenstown, Crovie, Rosehearty and Pennan. In some of them the houses stand gable end to the sea as protection against the rough weather and nestle below spectacular cliffs—havens for seabirds. All should not be missed. Inland from this coast is a variety of castles, some inhabited like Inchdrewer and Eden, or in ruins as are Pitsligo, Pittulie and Dundarg.

Depart from Banff on the A98 westwards. For those exploring by road take the B9139 to Portsoy. A pretty diversion is to take the B9038 to the coast and the fishing village of Whitehills. Many varieties of wading birds can be found along this sandy shoreline.

Whitehills is one of the smallest ports in Scotland to have kept its own fleet and daily market. The village is built around Knock Head and

76   Mary Mull, Whitehills fishwife complete with creel, 1949 (PB)

retains its nineteenth century air with the closely packed houses gable end on to the sea. Although fishing has been carried on here for centuries, much building took place during the nineteenth-century herring boom and the harbour dates only from 1900. It is unusual in that it is not local authority owned, but run by commissioners elected by the village ratepayers. This is supposedly the place where the grey rat entered Scotland, having swum ashore from a shipwreck. The fishwives from Whitehills would walk with their creels to the railway in order to travel to places inland to sell their fish. Mary Mull (76) was a typical Whitehills fishwife.

To the east of Knock Head is the old harbour of Blackpots, which served the brick and tile works for over 200 years, the site of which is now a caravan park. The brick and tile industry was built on the local glacial deposits of a black Jurassic clay brought during the Ice Age from Sutherland. Boyne Castle is a ruin reached from across a field by the Scotsmill pottery on the B3139. The pottery is in a mill dating from 1626. The castle was built by the Ogilvy family around 1580 but was forfeited with the rest of their estate for supporting Bonnie Prince Charlie. The castle was 108 by 78 feet in size and four storeys high with four towers.

Situated on the shore to the east of Whitehills, and reached from the caravan park, is the Red Well, a beehive shaped house built by the Romans to protect a well. Built to metric measurements this has recently been renovated. On the spring and autumn equinoxes the first rays of sunlight over Troup Head (10 miles to the east) illuminate the interior of the building whilst the surrounding countryside is still dark. This phenomenon has given rise to the suggestion that it is some form of ancient calendar.

Leave Whitehills on the B9021, turning right for Portsoy at the crossroads with the B9139. For those wishing to attempt to walk the line return to Tillynaught Junction, turn left off the A98 at Smiddyboyne (603637) on to the unclassified road. Since the trackbed is heavily overgrown at Tillynaught an easier joining place is the overbridge at 601629 on that unclassified road. The trackbed to Portsoy can be identified from the A98 by the two lines of parallel fences and walking most of it to the outskirts of Portsoy should be possible.

III

Tillynaught to Elgin

History of the section

As was noted in the previous section, the line from Tillynaught to Portsoy was part of the original GNSR Act, but circumstances forced an independent company to construct it. The GNSR finally absorbed the line in 1867.

By the 1880s the GNSR was in much better shape, physically and financially, and extensions along the coast were considered. The first scheme from the GNSR at that time for a railway along this coast was a slightly longer revival of the Portsoy to Port Gordon scheme abandoned in 1867, passing behind Cullen instead of along the shore at the foot of the cliffs. The lack of a through connection to Elgin was disliked locally and the Highland Railway offered an alternative from Keith to Buckie and Cullen. The GNSR responded with a proposal for a line all the way to Elgin.

On 12 July 1882 both the GNSR and Highland Railway Acts received the Royal Assent. The new GNSR line was to run from Portsoy to Lossie Junction on the Lossiemouth branch (Map 12). More of the Highland line will be found in the next section.

The original line to Portsoy was a branch off the line to Banff and ended in a small terminus station, which faced the sea, together with a steep branch to the harbour, which fell into disuse once the coast extension was opened. The extension started with a sharp curve just short of the old station, which became a goods depot. The $4\frac{1}{4}$ miles to Tochieneal opened on 1 April 1884, while the $7\frac{3}{4}$ miles from Lossie Junction to Garmouth opened on 12 August of the same year. The intervening $13\frac{1}{4}$ mile section contained some heavy works, including the embankments and viaducts at Cullen and the Spey viaduct. Goods traffic started on 5 April and passenger trains on 5 May 1886 with a formal opening on 1 May. On the same dates a loop was constructed between the mainline and the branch half a mile east of Grange station, eventually Cairnie Junction. This was to allow through running from

72

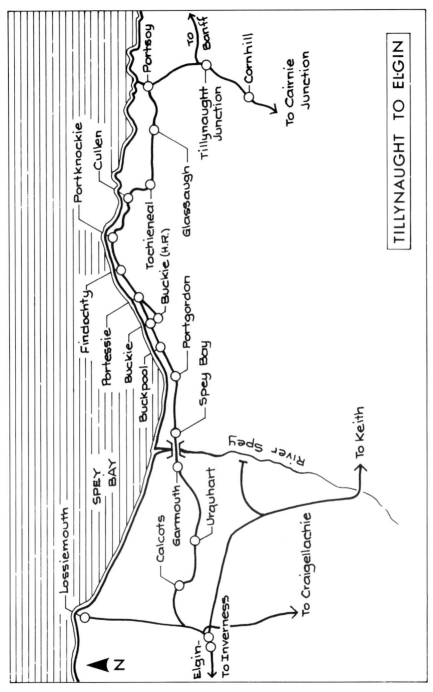

Map 12   Tillynaught to Elgin (GNSR)

Aberdeen without reversal at Grange station. Because the GNSR already owned the land it did not seek parliamentary approval, but had second thoughts and obtained permission in its Act of 19 July 1887.

The line was single track, except between Buckie and Portessie but the Act of 12 August 1898 authorised the doubling of the Elgin to Lossie Junction section. However, this was never carried out.

Originally trains for both the Craigellachie and coast sections were divided or joined at Huntly but on 1 June 1898 Cairnie Junction at the south end of the 1866 Grange South loop was opened.

Closure of this line to both passengers and freight occurred on 6 May 1968 when the, by then freight only, Banff branch also closed. Thus, unless otherwise stated, all the stations closed on 6 May 1968.

Portsoy 12m 65c.

For those travelling on the B9139 turn right onto the A98 in the outskirts of Portsoy. Those on the old trackbed are recommended to do the same as the line has been made impassable for the last part into Portsoy. A possible point of exit from the trackbed is the bridge over the B9022 at 591651. Follow the A98 (Aird Street) in to the town centre, just after the road turns sharp left and becomes Seafield Street look out for the tell-tale GNSR gates on the left, this is the entrance to the station and the park it has now become.

Portsoy Old station (590658, OS sheet 29, Banff)

This is a typical GNSR terminus trainshed building, as can be seen at Macduff, and is now in commercial use and thus preserved (77). To the west of the old station is the GNSR goods shed, still in use. This station opened on 30 July 1859, closing to passengers on 1 April 1884 and to freight on 6 May 1968 (78). The harbour branch (79 and 80), which can be seen on the right of the station building, probably closed when the coast line was built but it was not lifted until 1910. The branch is now part of the park and forms a grassy pathway down, under three bridges to the harbour and makes a very pleasant short walk. The tiny harbour is well worth seeing, as are the attractively restored buildings around (Map 13).

77   Portsoy Terminus Station (L&G)

78   Portsoy Terminus Station, looking north, August 1988 (RRFK)

79   Portsoy Harbour branch, looking north (L&G)

80   Portsoy Harbour branch, looking north, August 1988 (RRFK)

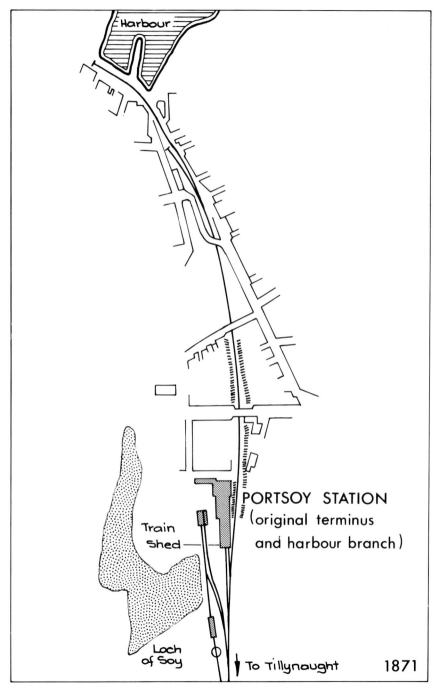

Map 13   Portsoy, old station and harbour branch

Portsoy New station (589657, OS sheet 29, Banff)

When the coast extension was built a very sharp curve had to be constructed here so that the new station (81) is at right angles to, and just in front of, the old. The new station consisted of a passing loop with two platforms joined by a footbridge, the main station building on the up side, a waiting shelter on down platform, and a signal box. Of this, only the main station building has survived, now being a green and cream painted Scout hut (82). It is of a larger style than most of the GNSR wooden stations, having two forward facing transverse extensions (Map 14).

Both the stations are set in a park which has been laid out on the station site, and contains an attractive lake. Within this park the line can be followed for a short way in both directions. Towards Tillynaught the trackbed curves sharply right and ends a little way past the children's playground. Towards Cullen the trackbed has been partly obliterated by the park but its course can be found again shortly before where new houses have been built over it.

Portsoy was created a burgh of barony for the Ogilvies of Boyne in 1550. One of the specialities of Portsoy is Portsoy Marble which is a beautiful variety of Serpentine of subtle green and reddish colouring. It is found in a vein running across the braes to the west of the harbour, near the new swimming pool. Patrick Ogilvie, Lord Boyne, developed the harbour in 1692 to export the marble, and it became very popular in France where Louis XIV used it for two of the chimneypieces in the Palace of Versailles. From 1700 until the Act of Union the importation of marble to Scotland was forbidden.

Portsoy's original harbour used to be one of the safest in the area and handled trade with England and the Continent. In 1825 Lord Seafield extended the harbour. Herring fishing contributed to that prosperity but that has all gone now. The harbour is used by creel boats, used for lobster and crab fishing, and pleasure sailing. Today the harbour walls and jetties are most likely to be occupied by seabirds of many types, including the impressive great skua.

Like many of the towns along this coast it has a wealth of seventeenth- and eighteenth-century buildings which have been restored and form the centrepiece of the award-winning conservation area. These include the Old Star Inn which dates from 1727 and Soy House, the oldest building in Portsoy.

Worth visiting are the marble workshop and pottery by the harbour, Boyne Castle, and the park which contains the remains of the railway station and Loch Soy. The latter was created by a dam to serve the paddle wheel of a now defunct oatmeal mill but it has been reduced in

81 Portsoy New Station, looking to Tillynaught (L&G)

82 Portsoy New Station, August 1988 (RRFK)

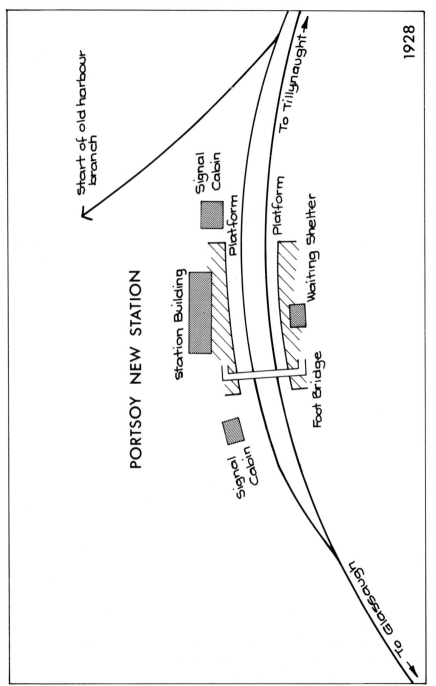

Map 14   Portsoy, new station

size, and now houses swans and paddle boats. Portsoy has a swimming pool amidst the rocks to the west of the harbour.

Portsoy has a variety of leisure facilities, including a swimming pool, sandy beaches, bowls, golf, horse riding, fishing (salmon, trout and sea angling), kart racing, sea cruises and a caravan park. Among the eating places is the 'Cup and Saucer' which has on its walls the story of the Glassaugh Windmill, known locally as the Cup and Saucer because of its shape.

Depart on the A98 towards Cullen. For those on foot the trackbed runs close to this road and places to rejoin can be found outside the town.

Glassaugh 14m 70c (559654, OS sheet 29, Banff)

Continue along the A98 and, just after the Glenglassaugh Distillery and the disused windmill alongside it, the station platforms are visible in a meadow on the left. Turn left onto the small track, which has a 'public right of way' notice slightly past the windmill (557655). This leads to the station site and at its end is a house called 'Sandygates' which was probably the staion house. For those on foot the trackbed from west of Portsoy will have been relatively easy walking, except where the bridges are out. Most of the land is rough grazing for cattle and sheep, that is, short grass with thistles and nettles. Look out for rabbits and brown hares.

Passing Sandygates on the left leads to the site of the level crossing which still has two gates and four posts. However, by keeping the house on the right one enters the station yard through a GNSR gate with a wheel at the end (83) and an LNER trespass sign (30).

Glassaugh had the smaller, more common, type of GNSR wooden station without the recess on the platform side (84), as can still be seen at Urquhart. On the opposite platform was a wooden waiting shelter, as still exists at Longmorn (see *Speyside Railways,* fig 3). All the station buildings have gone but both platforms and the loading bay are extant, (85, Map 15) and can easily be identified. On the north platform can be seen the base of the old station building. To the north of the station is a large station yard, probably for the traffic generated by the distillery.

Glassaugh was recorded as closed on 21 September 1953 and on 20 April 1964, so it presumably reopened sometime in between those dates.

The windmill, located on the site of a prehistoric burial mound, dates from 1761. It is listed a category B building of architectural and historic interest. It is currently being restored and its full history can be seen in

83   Wheeled GNSR gate at Glassaugh, August 1988 (RRFK)

the Cup and Saucer tearoom in Portsoy, the windmill being locally known as the cup and saucer because of its shape. Windmills are uncommon in the north east of Scotland.

Depart by either continuing along the clear trackbed to the west or by rejoining the A98 and turning left.

Before moving on, a worthwile detour is to Sandend and Fordyce. For Fordyce take the unclassified road to the left of the A98 at 555656 and for Sandend turn right a little further west at 554656.

Sandend is a nineteenth-century fishing village, beloved of artists. It is situated at the west end of a wide sandy bay which provides plenty of fun for children. Geologically, this is an area of marine silts and clays. Fish is still cured at Sandend and the fresh or smoked variety can be purchased there. A $1\frac{1}{2}$ mile cliff top path leads from Sandend to Findlater Castle. This was founded in 1455 and built into the face of the cliff as a fortress for the Ogilvies of Deskford. It was abandoned in the mid seventeenth century, but not before it had been visited by Mary Queen of Scots.

Fordyce is a very secluded village with narrow streets containing many historic and preserved buildings. The church was mentioned in 1272 and the ruins of old St Tarquin's Kirk, dating from 1661, have

84   Glassaugh, looking to Portsoy (WGD)

85   Glassaugh looking to Portsoy, August 1988 (RRFK)

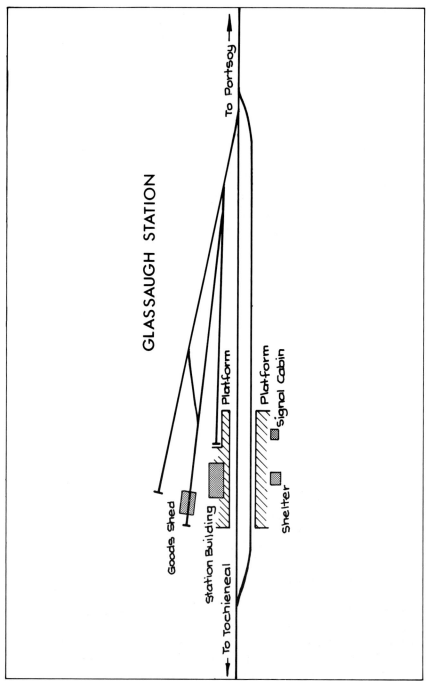

GLASSAUGH STATION

To Portsoy →

← To Tochieneal →

Goods Shed

Station Building

Platform

Platform

Signal Cabin

Shelter

Map 15   Glassaugh

been restored. These include a belfry with upstairs room equipped with a fireplace. In the churchyard are two canopied tombs. The castle is in the middle of the village and was built in 1592 by Thomas Menzies, an Aberdeen burgess. Its L-shaped plan, corbelled stair turret and crowstepped gables make it a prime example of the Scottish Baronial style of architecture. Overlooking the village is Durn Hill which has the remains of a Pictish fort.

Tochieneal 17m 11c (523657, OS sheet 29, Banff)

There should be no problem in walking from Glassaugh, certainly some of the bridges (e.g. that east of Dytach) are still in place. For those travelling by road turn left off the A98 at 522658 onto an unclassified road signposted to Lintmill. Cross the railway bridge and turn left passing railway gates and a railway cottage on each side.

The station originally consisted of the two platforms serving the two lines of the passing loop. The main building was the normal GNSR flat fronted wooden structure with a signal box on the same platform (86).

Again, with the exceptions of the houses, there are no station buildings to be seen but the rectangular concrete base of one of them is to be discovered on the southerly of the two long platforms. Between the platforms the area has been fenced to provide pens for various small animals and many beehives (87).

This station site is quiet and secluded and seems to be a haven for wild animals and birds, which were constantly discovered amongst the dense vegetation. There are many rabbits, and in a few moments may be seen chaffinches, swallows, linnets and other small birds, and, on a summer's day, many butterflies. In autumn one may find Scandinavian visitors such as fieldfares and redwings.

To the south of the platforms is an extensive area, probably for sidings, with a loading bay at the extreme south at the edge of an embankment (88). This has stone walls intact on the east and north sides and a roadway leads on to it from the west (Map 16). No other artifacts were readily discovered here but the houses were surrounded by good examples of paling fences (33). The goods yard and loading bay area is overgrown with all kinds of plants from Scots pines to the tiny eyebright. Fireweed, as usual, is in evidence, plus hawkweed, thistles, elderberry and alder. There is too some evidence of horticulture in the past as shown by the roses and even clumps of applemint.

Tochieneal station was recorded as having closed on both 1 October 1951 and 20 April 1964 so, like Glassaugh, it must have reopened sometime between those dates. Also shared in common with its neighbour

86   Tochieneal, looking to Glassaugh (AC)

87   Tochieneal, looking to Cullen, August 1988 (RRFK)

88   Loading dock at Tochieneal, August 1988 (RRFK)

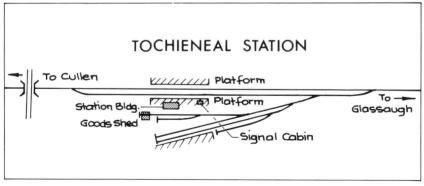

Map 16   Tochieneal

Glassaugh was the likelihood of extensive goods traffic, if the size of the yard is any indication. As at Glassaugh there was a distillery. This belonged to Alexander Wilson and had opened in 1822. However, in search of a better water supply he moved the distillery in 1871 to Inchgower to be served by the HR Rathven station.

Lintmill, the nearest village, was named after the flax growing and linen production started by Lord James Deskford, the son of the second earl of Seafield.

Leave, either along the trackbed to the west, which becomes more overgrown as one approaches Cullen, or return to the A98 and turn left.

Cullen 18m 29c (514673, OS sheet 29, Banff)

The station site has been built upon and the line to the south partly obliterated. For this reason walkers are advised to rejoin the A98 on the outskirts of Cullen.

Enter Cullen on the A98, Seafield Road, and head towards the sea. You are now looking down through one of the arches of the famous Cullen set of viaducts. To the right of the railway arch over this road is Station Road, which leads to a new housing estate called New View Court, built on the station site. Alternatively turn right into Seafield Place off Seafield Street (the A98) and stop just past Blantyre Street.

The building of the railway through Cullen involved a series of high embankments and brick and masonry arches and viaducts which divide the old seatown at Cullen from the upper town and which are one of the most spectacular features of the coast line. The curvaceous nature of the line was because the Earl and Countess of Seafield refused to let the railway cross the policies of Cullen House. The Earl was a director of the Highland Railway and never used the GNSR from Cullen, preferring to travel by road to Rathven station of the HR Portessie to Keith branch. He would request his guests to do the same (see section IV).

Cullen station was built on a curve where the line abruptly changed direction (89). The station building was wooden, of the same larger type as at Portsoy with two transverse sections through the main section, and was situated on a single curved platform facing east. There was no passing loop but several sidings and a two road goods shed (Map 17).

The new housing estate curves round with the line of the railway and at the Tillynaught end it is obvious where the new houses have been built between the two parallel rows of older properties which used to border the railway. From that point there is about 100 yards of clearly defined cutting going south (90) until the site of the former bridge over Seafield Place. The next 100 yards of the cutting to the south have been

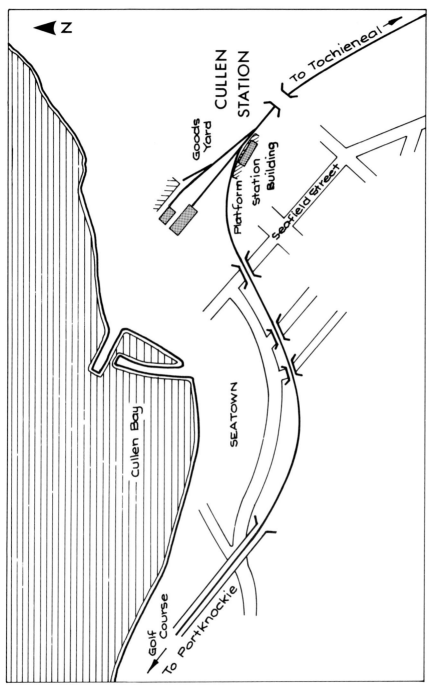

Map 17 Cullen

89   Cullen, looking to Portknockie (LOS)

90   Cullen, looking north, August 1988 (RRFK)

filled in and are used as a carpark. After that the cutting is visible but is heavily overgrown and almost certainly impassable. At the eastern end of the station site one house has been built almost on the end of the first viaduct.

The obstinacy of the Earl of Seafield meant the creation of the viaducts which are one of the great sights of this coast line and impart a special air to Cullen, framing some of the best views of this pretty little town. Starting at the eastern end there is a double arched viaduct, one arch of which crosses over the end of Seafield Street, almost like a gate in a city wall (91), then a four arched viaduct, (92) another single arch (by the Three Kings Hotel) and finally the eight-arch viaduct and crowning glory (93). The first and last of these have been effectively sealed off from the public but the other two can be accessed by climbing the sides of the intervening embankments and people do walk these. The townspeople consider the viaducts so much a feature of Cullen's landscape that they are currently opposing BR's threats to demolish these arches.

These magnificent structures are best seen from either the east end by the Bay Hotel or from the golf course at the west. Cullen used to be 'dry', so the Bay Hotel was built outside the town boundary so the fishermen could easily get a 'wee dram'.

91   Cullen Viaduct, over Seafield Street, August 1988 (RRFK)

92   Cullen Viaduct, August 1988 (RRFK)

93   Cullen Viaduct, August 1988 (RRFK)

Cullen is famous for the Three Kings Rocks. One is by the golf clubhouse and two on the foreshore. They are named after three kings killed in a battle on the beach with the Vikings. Cullen House, the property of the Seafields, lies to the south of the line and nearby is the cruciform church founded by Robert the Bruce.

The original village was Invercullen at the mouth of Cullen Burn. About 1300 the villagers were moved inland to what is now Old Cullen. It received its first charter in the thirteenth century. Between 1820 and 1830 the Earl of Seafield built a new town to the plans of George MacWilliam. Cullen has been a fishing village for at least five centuries and Seatown, with its narrow twisting streets of painted houses and probably built on the site on Invercullen, is the picturesque remains of that heritage, although the harbour is now mostly used by pleasure craft. Haddock was Cullen's speciality and three large curing houses were the basis of a thriving trade. Cullen Skink is a local delicacy, a fish soup based upon smoked haddock. A harbour was built in 1817 and enlarged in 1834. Soon it was exporting fish, timber, potatoes and oats and importing salt, barley and coal in addition to the fishing. Now the pleasure sailors have it to themselves.

The Ogilvies, who lived at Findlater Castle, built Cullen House close to the village and church in 1600. The owner of Cullen House became the Earl of Findlater in the seventeenth century and in the eighteenth century the house passed to the Earl of Seafield. The house was originally an L-shaped tower house, typical of north east Scotland. It was extended through additions of Robert Adam in 1711 and David Bryce in 1858. It had 386 rooms. In 1975 the Earl sold the house and contents and the house has subsequently been converted into flats.

Worth seeing in Cullen is the Auld Kirk, dedicated to the Virgin Mary, which was in the old town and dates from at least 1236 (the earliest record). Robert the Bruce's queen Elizabeth de Burgh, died in Cullen. Her interior parts are buried in this church and he endowed a chaplaincy to pray for her soul. The church was extended in 1536 with St Anne's Aisle on the south side, in 1602 with the Seafield Loft, a Laird's gallery, and 1798 by the north aisle. Also to be seen is the Market Cross in the market square. It originally stood in Old Cullen and dates from 1696, though it incorporates an older carving of the Blessed Virgin and the Holy Child.

Cullen has a variety of restaurants, cafés, pubs, accommodation, banks and shops for the tourist. It has a caravan and camping site and facilities for fishing, bowling, golf and walking.

Findlater Castle, perched on the cliff edge, can be reached by following the path eastwards along the shore from the harbour. It is about a 2½ mile walk. Deskford village and church, an ancient monument with a finely carved sacrament house dating from 1551, is four miles south of Cullen. The nearby Bin Hill, rising to 1,053 feet, is a favourite climb while a pleasant wooded walk is to Crannoch. For this take the track from Seafield Place above the caravan site and then fork right.

Leave Cullen either by the A98 towards Portknockie or on part of the trackbed from Cullen to Portknockie which has been made into a coast path. It can be joined off the A98 opposite the Cullen Bay Hotel or by walking along the beach, past the golf course to the end of the viaduct. Here there is a path up the embankment leading to the trackbed walkway.

Portknockie 20m 37c (486684, OS sheet 28, Elgin)

Either walk along the trackbed to Portknockie or follow the A98 turning right on to the A942.

The station was at the west of the town just before the A942 does a sharp left turn. The entrance is in Station Street and can be recognised by the GNSR station gates.

Portknockie station had staggered platforms (94) with the smaller type of flat fronted GNSR wooden station building on the east bound platform. All that remains is the platform on the south side (95) with the foundations of the building and a concrete notice post whilst a loading gauge is to be seen on the northern side (29 and Map 18). The trackbed has been filled in the centre of the station to provide access to the new houses beyond.

Portknockie originated as a fishing village around the natural harbour which is sheltered by Greencastle Hill to the north. As in most of these harbours pleasure craft have replaced the fishing boats. Because of the shortage of room at the water's edge the village grew on the clifftops overlooking the harbour, where possibly the magnificent views across to Caithness were some recompense for the winter's gales. The original houses were built gable end to the sea for protection from those gales. The later skippers' homes are behind these and laid out in a more conventional way. The natural harbour was improved in 1887–90 and another pier added in 1933. The railway and the harbour improvements caused a great increase in Portknockie's population in the last years of the last century and in 1912 the town became a burgh.

Portknockie has bowls, golf, tennis and a paddling pool. There are shops, banks, eating places and accommodation. The cottages are all well cared for, and much of the village is a conservation area.

Although there is little to be seen of the station at Portknockie one is rewarded all along this section by breathtaking views of the Moray

94   Portknockie, looking to Cullen, 21 October 1954 (JLS)

95   Portknockie, looking to Cullen, August 1988 (RRFK)

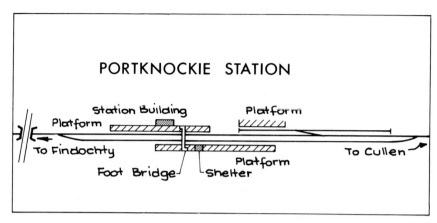

Map 18   Portknockie

Coast, one of the great sadnesses that this line ever closed. Doubtless had it managed to survive until now the pressures of tourism could have given it a new lease of life. On clear days the hills of Caithness can be seen across the sea. The highest one, which is slightly conical, is Morven, 2,313 feet high and 50 miles away. To the right of that and 25 miles away is Wick, but it is not visible as it is below the horizon. To the south can be seen the much nearer Bin of Cullen which rises to 1,050 feet.

The coastline in both directions from here has a spectacular array of cliffs and rocky coves. One of the most famous rock formations along this coast is Bow Fiddle Rock, situated to the east of the harbour (96). Walk a little across the grassy cliffs and you will discover this spectacular formation lying just offshore. Many small plants, including common yellow toadflax cover the cliffs, and seabirds, such as oystercatchers and herring gulls, can be observed nesting in the crevices.

Leave Portknockie either by following the trackbed, which is quite walkable with most of the bridges between here and Findochty in place, or take the A942 towards Findochty.

Findochty 21m 63c (466678, OS sheet 29, Elgin)

Walking along the trackbed will bring one to the site of Findochty station. If travelling by road the station site is just after the A942 makes a sharp right turn towards the sea.

Findochty has a single platform (Map 19) with a small type flat fronted GNSR wooden building with its back to the sea (97). On closure

96   Bow Fiddle Rock, Portknockie, August 1988 (RRFK)

the building was demolished but the platform and the GNSR lamposts remained until two years ago (98). Since then the whole site has sadly been levelled and nothing remains (99).

Findochty is pronounced 'Finnechtie' and, like most of the other villages along this coast, fish was the reason for its existence. The earliest reference to Findochty is in 1440. In 1568 the Ord family

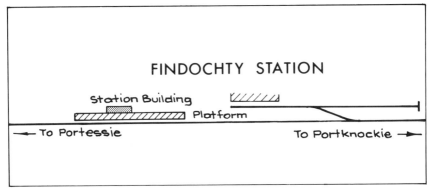

Map 19   Findochty

97   Findochty, looking east, 21 October 1954 (JLS)

98   Findochty, looking east, July 1985 (RRFK)

99   Findochty, looking east, August 1988 (RRFK)

acquired the manor, port, customs and fishers' lands of Findochty and in 1716 the local laird persuaded thirteen men and four boys to move from Fraserburgh to establish a new fishing station. In 1880 a new harbour was built and this, with the coming of the railway, made Findochty expand, it becoming a burgh in 1915. Eventually the fishing declined and the remainder transferred to Buckie so that Findochty harbour is the preserve of leisure sailors.

In the sixteenth century the Ords built a castle to the west of the village which is now a ruin. Near here in 961 was the Battle of the Bauds in which the Scots King Indolphus beat the Norsemen under Eric of the Bloody Axe.

Like so many of the fishing villages along this coast the houses are brightly painted in many colours. This is because oil paints, rather than whitewash, are used to protect them from the weather.

Findochty has bowls and golf, some shops and a caravan and camping park. There are marvellous cliff walks in both directions, and an old smugglers route can be followed to Buckie.

Depart either along the trackbed, or on the A942 towards Buckie.

Portessie 23m 19c (447667, OS sheet 28, Elgin)

Either continue along the trackbed where the walking will not be too bad or drive along the A942. At map reference 445667 turn left and follow the road to the top of the hill, Station Road is a turning on the left.

To the right the road passes over two bridges, immediately adjacent. The first crosses the GNSR and the second the HR trackbeds. Standing on this bridge and looking west one can see the two trackbeds diverging and the next pair of bridges, each characteristic of its company, which are much farther apart.

This station consisted of a platform on the northern side for GNSR Aberdeen bound trains and an island platform for GNSR Elgin trains and HR trains (100 and Map 20). The former had a standard smaller flat fronted GNSR station building and the latter a smaller wooden planked building of a larger type than the normal down platform waiting shed. It had a pitched roof compared with the sloping roof of the usual waiting shelter. The two platforms were joined by a footbridge.

Although the trackbed on either side of the station is walkable, in the station area it is heavily overgrown, especially on the HR trackbed. All that remains of this junction station are the platforms with the coping stones in place on the GNSR faces but missing on the HR side (101). However, despite its rather unpromising appearance, there are some finds to be made. There is some fencing and the remains of a gate on the northern platform and a small goods bay at its eastern end. To the north east of the station there are two more GNSR gateposts and three lamposts on the flight of steps leading down to the village and the sea (25). A variety of plants cover the station area including some bay bushes, gorse and knapweed, interspersed with raspberries, yarrow, clover, scabious and eyebright as well as brilliant yellow patches of celandine and buttercup.

Because HR trains ended their journeys here there used to be more facilities than at most stations along this route. These included a small engine shed, water tower (102) and turntable (103, Map 20). The stone base of the water tower can be seen on the south of the trackbed at the east end of the station. A yard or two past there is the heavily overgrown pit of the turntable. It is a 3 feet deep circular depression with a stone coping around its edge. South east of the turntable are the bases of the brick walls of the engine shed, almost abutting onto a small house. Portessie shed was unusual in that it was the only brick engine shed the Highland Railway possessed. It was closed in March 1909 but continued to exist for many years as a concrete block factory. Parts of the station site, especially round the turntable and HR area, are quite marshy and

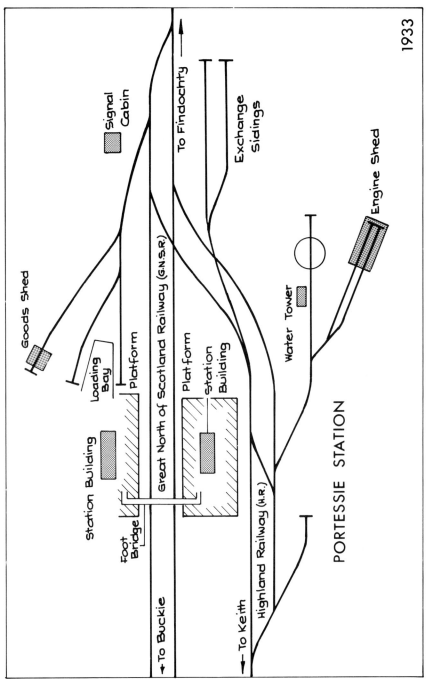

Map 20 Portessie

100   Portessie, looking east, 21 October 1954 (JLS)

101   Portessie, looking east, August 1988 (RRFK)

102   Base of Highland Railway water tower, Portessie, August 1988 (RRFK)

103   Highland Railway turntable pit, Portessie, August 1988 (RRFK)

support reeds, marestail, cotton grass, ferns and brackens and some spectacular varieties of fungus.

Mr Hay of Rannes founded Portessie as a fishing station in 1727 and, although proposals were made to build a harbour, none ever materialised. The original name of Portessie was 'Rottenslough' and occasionally it is still called 'The Sloch'. It was incorporated in the Burgh of Buckie in 1903.

Depart by either walking along the trackbed or returning to the seafront and turning left towards Buckie.

Buckie 24m 35c (429658, OS sheet 28, Elgin)

Walkers will find their way obstructed by an oil storage depot which has been built across the tracks immediately east of the station. Leave the trackbed where March Street, a small cul de sac off the A942, abuts the line of the railway and walk to the main road and turn left for 100 yards. Drivers will find the best place to park is on the left of the A942 between the oil depot and the fish merchants.

Buckie station was built between the coast and the low cliffs on top of which lies the town. The line had been double track from Portessie and Buckie station possessed a fine stone station building (104) with two transverse sections with gable ends facing the platform at the ends. The roof over the centre section extended in front of the building to provide some shelter and a wooden and glass partition provided some more. There was a GNSR wooden signal box on the northern up platform. On the southern side was a more substantial than average wooden building with a pitched roof. A roadway sloped down from the west to the shelter on the south platform and later the tracks were crossed by a girder footbridge placed on stone pillars which gave access from both platforms to the town (Map 21).

Sadly all has now gone with the exception of the two platforms and the steps on the north side, although the site of the steps on the other platform can be seen (105). This station site is very different from the others described in this book as it lies in the heart of an industrial area and the docks. Although much has been built over, it is possible to walk along the trackbed up to the bridge over North High Street. This had been bricked up and the cutting between there and the bridge at Cluny Terrace filled in and grassed over. The ground and the vegetation are rough, only hardy seaside plants and brambles, ivy and gorse surviving. The trackbed further to the west can be accessed from either Railway Terrace or West Cluny Terrace which are either side of the cutting west of Cluny Terrace. For travellers by road, turn left onto the A942.

104   Buckie, looking west (LOS)

105   Buckie, looking west, August 1988 (RRFK)

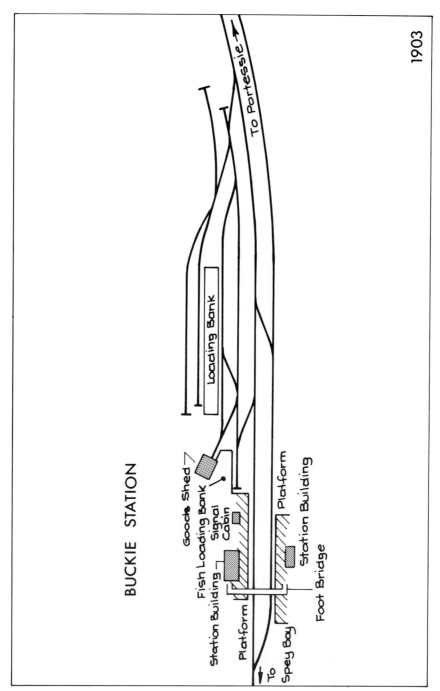

Map 21   Buckie (GNSR)

The first recorded reference to Buckie was in 1362. In the eighteenth and nineteenth centuries it grew and absorbed nearby villages. Greater Buckie, i.e. the inclusive area from Nether Buckie (or Buckpool which joined with Buckie Burgh in 1888) to Portessie (added to the Burgh of Buckie in 1903) was the largest town in the old county of Banff. While being less tourist orientated than some of the smaller communities along the coast, it has a wide variety of facilities for the tourist including many churches (often of architectural note), shops, eating places, banks, swimming pool, bowls, golf, squash, caravan and camping park, parks and play areas and a small, but helpful, Tourist Information Office. Buckie also has the annual gala and raft race and the flower show.

Fishing was very important here and Mr Gordon of Cluny opened a harbour here in 1880, built at a cost of £65,000 and covering 9 acres. The fishing trade grew greatly from that time and the sailing and row boats were replaced by steam drifters. In 1908 the town council bought the harbour and extended it over the following twenty years until it reached its present size. Sadly the fishing industry went into a decline and there is only a shadow of the former fishing activity present now. However, the Buckie fish market still operates every morning when fish is available, with Thursdays and Fridays being the busiest. Boat building and repairs are still carried on along this part of the coast.

Along the coastal areas of greater Buckie there are a large number of fishermen's houses, some with much outside architectural detail. The upper storeys were designed as net storage with outside access, although many have had these converted to bedrooms.

The Buckie Maritime Museum and Peter Anson Art Gallery house a collection relating to the fishing industry and other aspects of the history of Buckie. Buckie is on the Fishing Heritage Trail. The seamen's memorial in New Street and the war memorial in the Square are well worth visiting. Just south of the A98, a mile from Buckie, is the Leitcheston Doo'cot. It has four compartments and was built in the seventeenth century to provide fresh pigeon meat and eggs to the castle once nearby.

Walks along the shore either east or west (especially at the mouth of the Gollachy Burn) will reward one with the sight of many seabirds and waders. By taking the 'Winding Walk' from Queen Street along the Buckie Burn, the smaller birds of the area can be observed. Depart westwards along the coast road.

Buckpool 25m 41c (413653, OS sheet 28, Elgin)

Drive along the coast road, turning right onto the A990. Note the footbridge over the trackbed between Buckie and Buckpool (12 and 13).

This station was originally called Nether Buckie, the change of name being minuted on 25 November 1886. It closed on 7 March 1960. It consisted of a single platform with a recessed fronted GNSR wooden building on the northern side of the track (106). There was no passing loop, but a yard entered from the west served a loading bay. This had two sidings, one of which passed through a goods shed (Map 22).

Nearly all of this has gone under a housing development. Only the west end of one platform is now visible (107).

A harbour was constructed here in 1857 by Sir Robert Gordon of Letterfourie and the Board of Fisheries. Until then the fishermen had simply beached their boats on the shingle. However, the new harbour silted up very readily because of the effects of the fast flowing Spey estuary not very far to the west. It has now been filled in and landscaped into a pleasure park. In 1886 there was a dispute over which should be called 'Buckie harbour', Nether Buckie or Cluny which resulted in Nether Buckie harbour and its village both being renamed Buckpool.

The track to Portgordon is walkable, or continue driving west along the A990, noting the little two arch viaduct over a small burn at 405641 (36).

Portgordon 26m 73c (394642, OS sheet 28, Elgin)

Drivers should follow the A990. When it turns sharply left and inland at 392643, turn left immediately after the abutments of the dismantled overbridge.

Walkers will know that they are at Portgordon when the trackbed suddenly becomes a children's playground. Beyond that is a bowls green which occupies the site of the old station (108).

Portgordon station used to consist of a single platform with the ubiquitous recessed front GNSR wooden station building (109 and Map 23). Unlike the majority of stations on this line however, the building was on the southern side of the track. There was no passing loop but four sidings facing the down direction. During the Second World War three German spies came ashore nearby and tried to catch a train from Portgordon station. They were arrested, tried and the two male spies shot.

106   Buckpool, looking west, 21 October 1954 (JLS)

107   Buckpool, looking west (RRFK)

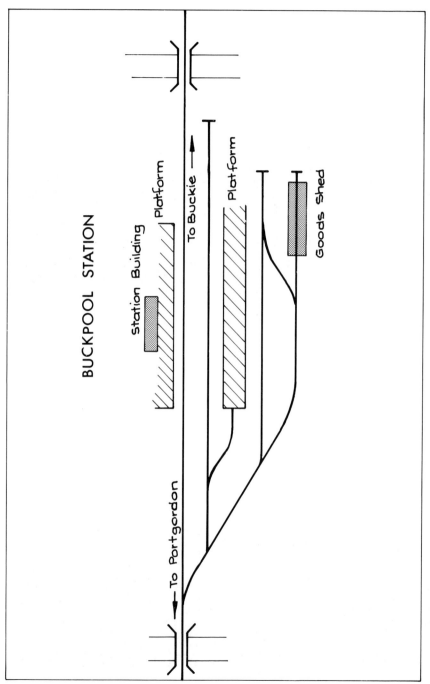

Map 22   Buckpool

108 Portgordon, looking west, August 1988 (RRFK)

109 Portgordon, looking west, 21 October 1954 (JLS)

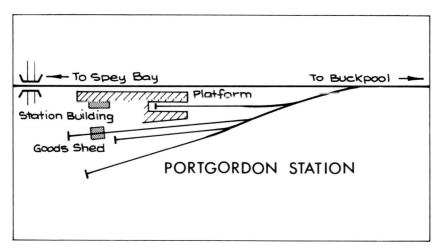

Map 23   Portgordon

The village was founded in 1797 and named after the Duke of
Richmond and Gordon who, in 1874, constructed a harbour. For
many years it was more important than Buckie with a substantial trade
exporting grain and importing salt and coal. Later herring fishing
became the staple trade until that also departed.

A long beach of sand and shingle stretches from Tannachy at the west
end of Portgordon to the Spey estuary and from which the stakes for the
salmon nets and their attendants can be seen.

Just to the east of Portgordon is the restored Gollachy Ice House,
originally built in 1834 to store ice with which to pack salmon caught
in the summer for shipment.

Two miles south of Portgordon is St Gregory's, the first post-
reformation Roman Catholic Church to be built looking like a church.
It was constructed in 1788, five years after the Catholic Relief Act,
although Preshome had been a secret administrative centre for
Catholics in northern Scotland. Just north of the A98 between
Portgordon and Fochabers is St Ninians Chapel Tynet. This was a
sheep-cote which was clandestinely used by Catholics and then given to
them in 1755 for use as a Chapel by the Laird of Tynet. It is known as
the Banffshire Bethlehem.

Either walk westwards along the trackbed or return to the seafront
and turn left on to an unclassified road. Just west of Portgordon one
crosses from Banffshire into Morayshire at the Burn of Tynet. Fossil
fish have been found in the Old Red Sandstone of the river valley. To
the south is Ben Aigan, 1,544 feet.

Spey Bay 29m 26c (355642, OS sheet 28, Elgin)

The walk to Spey Bay is possible but, because of the undergrowth, it may be heavy going in some places. The unclassified road crosses the old line at Porttannachy where good views of the line to Portgordon (110) and Spey Bay can be obtained across fields growing the traditional crops of oats and clover. Follow this unclassified road until it meets the B9104 and turn right. Spey Bay station is on the right where the road rises up to cross the line, with the entrance on the north of the line.

Spey Bay was originally called Fochabers-on-Spey until November 1893, then Fochabers until 1 January 1916 and then Fochabers and Spey Bay until 1 January 1918. Until the opening of the HR Fochabers branch the Highland had a station on its mainline also called Fochabers which, when the HR opened its branch to Fochabers (see *Speyside Railways*), became the junction for the branch and was renamed Orbliston Junction. Both these stations were four miles away from the town, one to the north and one to the south!

Spey Bay consisted of two platforms (111) a recessed front GNSR wooden station building on the Aberdeen bound platform. On the down platform was the usual shelter situated at the foot of the footbridge.

110   View to Portgordon from road bridge at Porttannachy, August 1988
(RRFK)

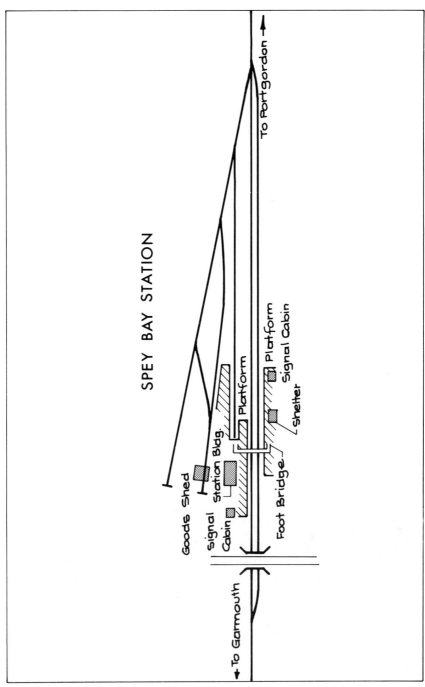

Map 24   Spey Bay

A signal box was to be found at the east of the down and at the west end of the up platforms (Map 24). Three sidings facing Buckie were provided. One entered a loading dock and one passed the other side of that into a goods shed.

The station building is still extant, but has been modified to be a garage at one end and at the other to hold a billiard table belonging to the man who lives in the old station house nearby. The building is made of horizontal boards painted cream above brown and has on its outside wall a drinking fountain inscribed 'T. Kennedy, patentee of Kilmarnock'. At the northern end of the station is the mark where a circular clock used to be. If one goes to the back of the station, and the garage is open, one can see on the inner wall the mark of the long case clock which obviously operated hands on faces in and outside the building, a common mechanism. There is also a GNSR lamp bracket on the building. To the east can be seen the goods bay and on the other platform the remains of the base of the signal box (1 and 112). The track is in parts heavily wooded with silver birch and conifers. The immediate environs of the station are covered in many types of wildflowers including knapweed, vetch, birds-foot trefoil, harebells, stitchwort and ragwort—a lovely sight in summer.

From here rejoin the B9104 and head towards Spey Bay to see the estuary and Tugnet Ice House. The fast waters of the Spey cause the shingle banks to continually shift; the river no longer flows under the central span of the viaduct. On three occasions, the last being in 1962, it has been necessary to cut a new channel for the river mouth as longshore drift has created long shingle banks. The large spit to the east is appropriately called Tugnet and from it salmon netting is carried out. Many methods of keeping the salmon during transit had been tried but fresh ice was the best. The ice was collected from special nearby ponds. The ice house is the largest in Scotland and was built in 1830 to contain ice for packing the salmon. It has been restored and contains an exhibition as part of the Fishing Heritage Trail.

Besides the ice house, there are super views of the Spey estuary and viaduct with the mountains (Ben Rinnes, 2,755 feet, and Ben Aigan, 1,544 feet) behind to be had from here (113). Around the estuary can be seen sea ducks, gulls, oystercatchers, kittiwakes, fulmars, cormorants, sandpipers, curlews, teal and ringed plovers. One might even be lucky enough to spot an osprey fishing in the estuary, or a seal. Spey Bay is the northern terminus of the 60 mile long Speyside Way. Also at Spey Bay is a hotel providing meals. Gliding, tennis and golf are also available at Spey Bay.

111   Spey Bay, looking east (JLS)

112   Spey Bay, looking east, August 1988 (RRFK)

113   Mountains from Tugnet Ice House, August 1988 (RRFK)

Spey Viaduct (348643, OS sheet 28, Elgin)

Even if one is travelling by road there is no excuse not to walk across the viaduct. One can either follow the Speyside Way to the bridge or return on the B9104 to take the very sharp right turn immediately after crossing the line. This leads to the end of the bridge where one can park. The banks of the river here are stoney and support much vegetation, including gorse and other shrubs and indian balsam, buttercups and ladies bedstraw in abundance during the summer months. As is the case along much of its length, the Spey here attracts many anglers. It is also possible to see the distinctively shaped boats used by the salmon fishers who net the salmon as they come upstream.

   The pathway leads across the bridge (114) to the site of Garmouth station, again giving superb views of the Spey and the mountains. The viaduct has a total length of 950 feet with a central bow arch girder span of 350 feet. At the time of its construction in 1886 it was one of the largest in Great Britain.

   The Spey, at 110 miles, is the second longest river in Scotland, and is said to be the fastest flowing of any river in the country. One of the finest salmon rivers in Scotland, it rises near the Corriyarrick Forest.

114   Spey Viaduct, looking southwest, July 1987 (RRFK)

The walk across the viaduct is a pleasant one, offering, apart from the obvious engineering interest, splendid views of the river and of the hills to the south. The lineside beyond the viaduct has many undisturbed flowers and animals. In amongst the grasses can be found many varieties of small butterflies and their caterpillars as well as typical plants including gorse, bell heather, knapweed, brackens and rosebay willow herb. Many sea and estuary birds may be found feeding in the marshy channels where the Spey has forsaken its old routes, and there are large breeding colonies of Arctic and Common Terns on the shingle.

If on the road, return to the B9104 and go to Fochabers, turning right outside the town onto the A96 to Elgin. Fochabers has several interesting things to see, including the old HR station (see *Speyside Railways*), Baxters preserve factory and visitors' centre, the folk museum, Christie's Garden Centre, Bellie Kirk (1798) with the Georgian houses around it, the Victorian Milne's High School (1846) and a range of shops and eating places as well as bowls, golf, tennis, swimming and fishing. Gordon Castle, to the north of the town, is not open to the public but is a Georgian House with a battlemented façade nearly 200 yards long and with 365 windows.

To the south east of Fochabers is the Speymouth Forest, through which there are attractive walks. Within this forest live roe deer and red squirrels, although because of their shyness they can be difficult to see. On the closeby moors are capercailzie, grouse, tawny owls and kestrels.

Garmouth 30m 45c (355640, OS sheet 28, Elgin)

Continue west along the A96 until the crossroads with the B9015, where
one turns right. The bridge over the line is still in place and obvious.
Immediately after crossing it turn sharp left. The site of the station was
on the left, just past the entrance to the Spey Viaduct walk, which starts
to the west of the bridge taking the B9015 over the trackbed.

This station was double track at one time but soon was singled as an
early plan (Map 25) indicates two platforms and two tracks while an
early photograph shows two platforms but only one track (115). Later
photographs show only one platform (116). The station consisted of a
standard flat fronted GNSR wooden building, like most of the others
on this line, situated on the northern side. Whether this was because of
the weather or because it was the up, Aberdeen bound, side and
Aberdeen was the headquarters of the GNSR we know not. A signal
box and two sidings used to be at the eastern end.

Once again all this has vanished, with part of the site occupied by a
housing development. At least that is appropriately called 'The Sidings'.

The rest of the site is heavily overgrown (117) but the platforms can
be located with care and many nettle stings.

From here to the west the track is heavily overgrown and we would
recommend going by road for some distance. Leave Garmouth on the
unclassified road in a westerly direction. The countryside from here to
Elgin is undulating arable land growing crops of oats, turnips and
barley, interspersed with clumps of deciduous and pine trees, full of
wood pigeons and starlings. On a clear day there are good views inland
to the hills.

Garmouth was founded by the Innes family and created a burgh of
barony in 1587. On the last Sunday in June is the Maggie Fair which
celebrates the latter. It is named after Lady Margaret Kerr who married
Sir James Innes and who, as heiress to the Duke of Roxburgh, brought
the Dukedom to the Innes family.

It was at Garmouth on 23 June 1650 that King Charles II, returning
from exile, landed and, against his will, signed the Solemn League and
Covenant as the price for his recognition as King by the Scots. However,
Charles considered that he was forced to sign it under duress and thus
ignored it. The place where he signed is identified by a plaque on a
cottage in the village. Garmouth used to be a port but the changes in the
river became too frequent for it to be of any use.

Near Garmouth is the village of Kingston-on-Spey. The fact that
Charles II came ashore in this area is not the reason for the name. The
village was founded as a ship-building centre in 1784 by two
Yorkshiremen who named it after Kingston-upon-Hull. They had

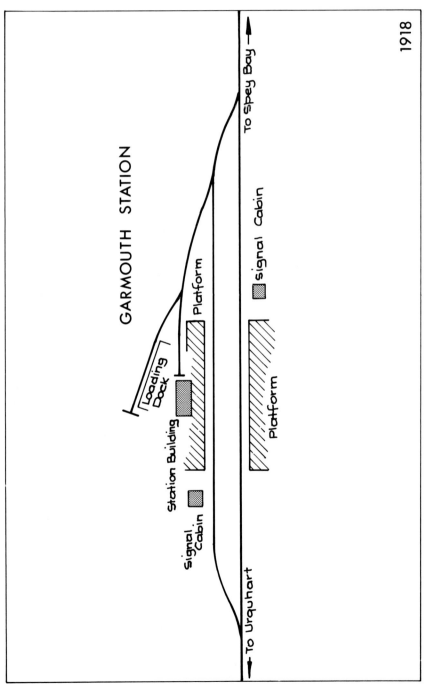

Map 25   Garmouth

115   Garmouth, looking west (LOS)

bought the extensive Forest of Glenmore and floated the timber down
the river. The ship building has now totally vanished. The oldest
building in Kingston is Dunfermline House, built by the monks of
Urquhart House, a daughter house of Dunfermline Abbey.

Urquhart 33m 65c (287631, OS sheet 28, Elgin)

Continue along this road and pass over the line on a bridge at 317629,
which still proclaims on a plate that it was made by 'James Abernethy
& Co. Engineers, Aberdeen, 1883'. From the bridge the overgrown
state of the trackbed in both directions can be clearly seen, as can the
little tunnel to the west (313628). Proceeding westwards one can see that
the bridges over the line at Lochs Crofts are still in place.

At the crossroads at 289622 turn right. A little after the village is the
station on the left of the overbridge.

Urquhart had another of the smaller GNSR wooden buildings of the
flat fronted type, but this time on the southern side of the tracks (118).
It was a single platform station, which is still extant, and had three
sidings and a goods shed (Map 26).

116   Garmouth, looking west to Elgin, 11 August 1954 (JLS)

117   Garmouth, looking west, August 1988 (RRFK)

118   Urquhart, looking west to Elgin, 11 August 1954 (JLS)

119   Urquhart, looking west, August 1988 (RRFK)

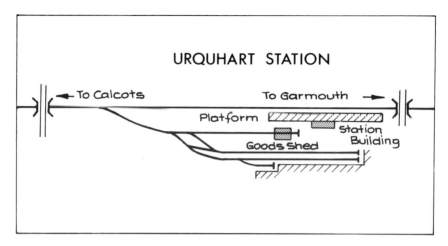

Map 26   Urquhart

We are in luck as the building has survived as the headquarters for a caravan site (2 and 119). It sits on the platform, a sight for sore eyes after some of the devastation we have seen. From the bridge the scene as it was in the days of steam can easily be imagined.

Here was a mediaeval Benedictine priory but, with the exception of a wheel cross in the wall of the church hall, all trace of it has vanished. It was founded in 1136 by David I and eventually was absorbed into Pluscarden Abbey.

North east of the crossroads at 640290 is a stone circle and north east of that are Innes House gardens, which are open to the public. South of Urquhart on the A98 is Lhanbryde. This means the church of St Bride or Bridget. It is a pretty little village with an interesting churchyard. On the B9103, south west of Lhanbryde is the Coxton Tower. It was built to withstand any attack short of artillery and was completed in 1644 by Sir William Innes. Visits are by appointment only. Telephone Lhanbryde 2225.

Leave Urquhart station by heading north away from the village and turn left at 287633, taking one past the church which is prominent on the skyline. Follow this track until one has recrossed the line and turn very sharply right underneath the track.

Calcots 36m 17c (256642, OS sheet 28, Elgin)

Follow the unclassified road until it meets the B9103 and turn left. The station is a quarter of a mile further on. Just past a house there is an entrance on the right which looks like a farm track, that is the old trackbed, the overbridge having been demolished. The trackbed from here to Elgin is nearly impassable, either because of undergrowth or because it has been ploughed out.

Calcots station (120) was a passing place with two platforms with the flat fronted GNSR building reverting to the northern up platform after the aberration at Urquhart. On the down side was a conventional waiting shelter and a signal box at the eastern end of the platform. To the north west was the station house. Two sidings were on the north side facing east (Map 27).

Again most of this has gone. The station house, slightly altered remains as does the up platform alongside the track (121) but very little else. All the station buildings have gone and the down platform has been levelled to increase the size of the field. Continue south on the B9103.

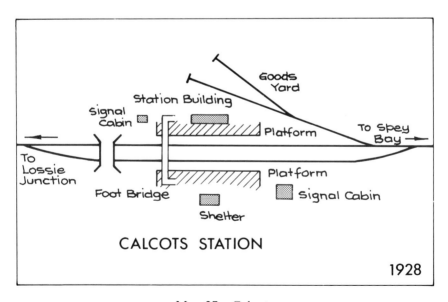

Map 27   Calcots

120   Calcots, looking to Elgin, 11 August 1954 (JLS)

121   Calcots, August 1988 (RRFK)

Lossie Junction 39m 09c (230637, OS sheet 28, Elgin)

Turn on an unclassified road at 254638 and about a mile and a half later turn left (240634). Just after the road crosses the railway (236644) turn left at a crossroads. Park where the bridge carrying the Lossiemouth line used to be.

Lossie Junction was a simple junction with no loops, just the line dividing into two, with a signal box (122), but it and most of the remains of the railway lines to the north and east have gone (123), although the line of the coast line can be seen curving away. It has been incorporated into a field, the edge of which marks the line. The bridge to the north east at 236644 can be seen in the distance. Careful searching will reveal the base of the signal box and the remains of a signal. To the south the cutting continues some way until past the unclassified road. After that the line has disappeared in an industrial estate. Continue on into Elgin.

Elgin 40m 25c (221622, OS sheet 28, Elgin)

Continue into the centre of Elgin crossing the A96 (to the east along the A96 is the site of the Pinefield crossing, just to the west of two garages, but now completely obliterated by the new development), and reach the station.

The station building (124) is in very good condition and largely unaltered, thanks to it being a listed building. It is being used as a freight headquarters. Do obtain permission before wandering around the station. Walk to the east end of the station and round the back where one can gain access to the platform, from whence it is possible to walk through to the Highland station. The through GNSR platform, the circulating area and the glass canopies (41) over these are still extant (Map 28). However, the terminal platforms and their canopies at the east of the station have gone for the benefit of the freight which also still uses the wooden goods shed at the eastern end of the old terminal platforms. Although battered, this shed retains its cream and brown livery. The yard seemed to be very busy and handling some container traffic from the south (see *Speyside Railways*).

The large signal box opposite the platform is still in use. The beautiful booking hall with its original woodwork and stained glass is in excellent condition and looked as if it has recently been redecorated (125). Note particularly the polished wood barriers by the former ticket windows, and, looking up, the elaborate plaster pendants hanging from the glazed vaulting.

122   Lossie Junction, looking north. Coast line to right, Lossiemouth branch
ahead, 1 March 1961 (JLS)

123   Lossie Junction, looking north, August 1988 (RRFK)

124   Elgin Station (GNSR) July 1987 (RRFK)

The first known mention of Elgin is in 1190. The mediaeval town plan of Elgin is still discernable. The High Street forms an axis to the town. It runs, widening from Lady Hill in the west to the cathedral in the east and it still contains some of the arcaded houses. On Lady Hill was a royal castle, occupied in 1296 by Edward I of England, but that has now gone and in its place is a tall column in memory of the Duke of Gordon who died in 1836.

In the market place is a Muckle Cross erected in 1650 and restored in 1888 by a native of Elgin. On the south side of the High Street is a hotel which was Thunderton House. In 1746 the Young Pretender, Bonnie Prince Charlie, used it as his headquarters when he spent eleven days in the town before the battle of Culloden. The little cross at the east end of the High Street marks the old boundary between town and cathedral lands.

Elgin Cathedral, the 'Lantern of the North', has had a chequered history. In the fourteenth century Bishop Barr called it the 'ornament of the district, the glory of the Kingdom and the admiration of foreigners'. It was built in 1224 and burnt down in 1390 by the Wolf of Badenoch whom the Bishop had excommunicated. It was rebuilt with a central tower but this collapsed in 1506. Again restored, the lead was removed from the roof in 1567 to pay for troops, the beautiful rood

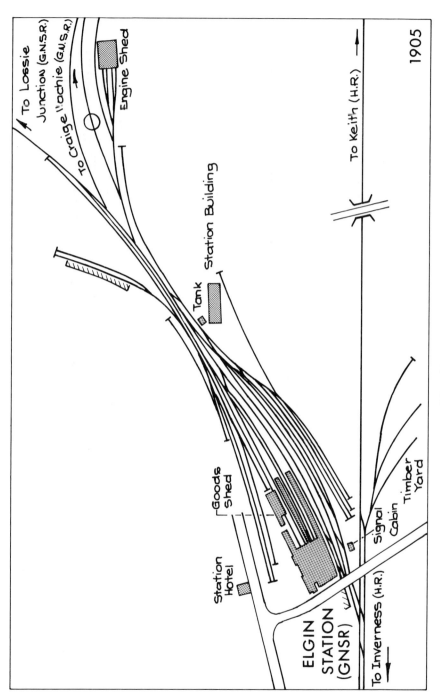

To Lossie Junction (G.N.S.R.)

To Craige l'achie (G.U.S.R.)

Engine Shed

To Keith (H.R.)

Station Building

Tank

Goods Shed

Station Hotel

ELGIN STATION (GNSR)

Signal Cabin

Timber Yard

To Inverness (H.R.)

1905

Map 28   Elgin

125   Elgin booking hall, July 1987 (RRFK)

screen was torn out in 1640 and Cromwell's troops smashed the tracery in the west windows. It has been allowed to decay since 1771. When complete the cathedral was nearly 300 feet long with towers at the west end 84 feet high. The remains are now in the care of the Government who are stopping any further deterioration and have provided a helpful information centre. The octagonal chapter house has been restored and re-roofed. Adjacent is the Bishop's House. The Cathedral and the Bishop's House are approached through well-tended Cooper Park, which also contains the elegant library with a collection of Morayshire photographs, including some of the GNSR.

Also worth seeing in Elgin or nearby are The Elgin Museum, Braco's Banking House, Masonic Close, Old Mills watermill and visitors' centre, Dr Gray's Hospital, Spynie Palace (formerly the seat of the Bishops of Moray but uninhabitated since the end of the seventeenth century and now a ruin) and churchyard. Duffus Castle at Old Duffus and Pluscarden Abbey. The latter is a Cistercian Abbey and is situated on Eildon Hill, which can be seen to the south west. It was founded in 1230 but fell into disuse after the reformation. The Benedictine community was able to take up residence again after nearly 400 years in 1948. Not far to the west is the original Dallas.

Thus the City of Elgin, with many shops, restaurants, hotels and facilities for golf, swimming, fishing, bowls and tennis, makes an excellent centre—situated between the coast and the countryside.

IV

Keith to Portessie

History of the section

When, in 1881, the GNSR proposed an extension from Portsoy to Portgordon the failure to go all the way to Elgin angered the local residents as it would mean no direct route to Inverness. The Highland Railway stepped in with a proposal for a line from Keith to the coast at Buckie and then to the east as far as Cullen. The next year the GNSR returned with a bill for a line all the way to Elgin which received parliamentary approval. Because of this the Highland bill was reduced to a line ending at Portessie but with running powers to Portsoy in the east and Buckie in the west, a total of $11\frac{1}{2}$ miles (Map 29). In return the GNSR was given running powers for $12\frac{1}{2}$ miles over the Highland between Elgin and Forres. It would seem that because the HR did not exercise its running rights, the GNSR were never able to use their reciprocal right. That was probably because the HR saw the danger of the GNSR getting to Forres, less than 25 miles from the centre of the Highland Railway at Inverness, and where there were also connections to the south on the HR line via Dava.

The first turf was cut on 7 November 1882 and the branch opened on 1 August 1884. Traffic was very light, the heaviest being for the annual Peter Fair at Rathven when extra trains were run, and the line was closed as a war economy on 9 August 1915. After a short while the $2\frac{1}{2}$ miles from Buckie to the distillery at Aultmore via Crooksmill siding was re-opened. The $1\frac{1}{2}$ miles between the HR station at Buckie and the junction with the GNSR at Portessie was also re-opened for the fish traffic, but operated by the GNSR. For a short period this working was extended to Rathven. Because of the lack of passing loops and the entrances to the sidings the trains were made up with wagons for Buckie behind the engine and those for Rathven in front. The closure of the distilleries by the government meant the end for even these truncated freight services. In 1917 the Admiralty requisitioned the track between Aultmore and Portessie.

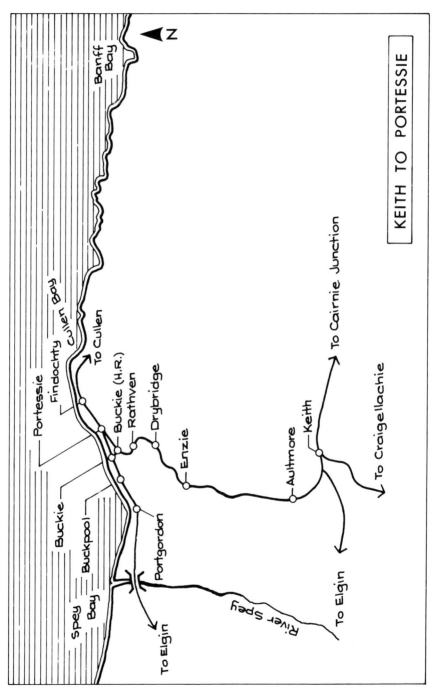

KEITH TO PORTESSIE

Map 29   Keith to Portessie (HR)

The buildings etc remained untouched as it was intended to re-open the line after the war. Highland freight services to Aultmore resumed in 1919 and the GNSR, using HR materials, relaid the Portessie to Buckie section and recommenced freight operations over that part of the line the same year. However, the line had still not been relaid and opened for freight throughout or at all for passengers when the Highland became part of the LMSR in 1923. The reluctance to relay the track may have been related to the very light traffic it had produced and the large increase in operating costs during the war. However, it is believed that the line was relaid using ex-Midland Railway chairs during the first two years of the LMSR. In spite of that, traffic was never resumed and the 10 miles from the distillery at Aultmore to Buckie were again lifted, this time during 1937. Eventually the herring traffic declined and the Buckie to Portessie section was closed officially on 1 April 1944, but it had almost certainly ceased well before then. The Keith to Aultmore section survived to serve the distillery until 3 October 1966.

All the buildings were typical Highland Railway wooden structures on stone foundations. Portessie, because it was a GNSR station, was the exception and had GNSR station buildings with HR water tower and engine shed. When the LMSR relaid the track it provided LMSR timetable boards.

With the exception of its two extremities, the line ran through a very thinly populated area and had to climb to 840 feet above sea level. However, when it first opened it had a monopoly of direct rail connections with Inverness and the initial service was four trains a day with an extra train on Wednesdays and Saturdays being added in the 1890s. After the first two years of its life it lost that monopoly position with the advent of the GNSR coast line which seems to have taken its toll because by the time the line closed there was only three services per day, taking between 35 minutes and an hour.

The junction at Keith faced away from Inverness which made through running to Inverness or the south difficult and, with the exception of special express Buckie to Liverpool and Manchester fish trains at the height of the herring seasons between 1885 and 1897, this did not occur.

The line was normally worked on the one engine in steam principle so that the passing loops, which had been installed at Enzie and Aultmore, were superfluous. In 1907 the intermediate signal boxes were closed, the signals removed, the points worked by hand and the loops removed.

Keith Junction 14m 42c (430516, OS sheet 28, Elgin)

Enter Keith on the A95, turn on to the B9116 and follow the signs to the station.

This station was the furthest west the GNSR went on the direct Aberdeen to Inverness route. The station still sees regular traffic with trains between those cities calling there. In addition there is an extensive goods yard and a considerable amount of freight traffic is handled.

At Keith station the GNSR and HR platforms formed the two sides of a vee with the station buildings at the broad end. For transfer traffic there was a long through platform where trains were handed over from one company to another. This has a windshield on the north side of the track, partially supported by girders from the canopy (126). At the east of the station were two GNSR bay platforms with steel and glass canopies and finally the station was completed by a curving platform to the south for the GNSR's line to Dufftown which curves away to the south west and rises steeply from the mainline (127, Map 30, see *Speyside Railways*).

When the HR Portessie branch was first opened, branch trains used the western end of the single through platform which the Highland

126　Keith interchange platform between GNSR and HR, looking to Aberdeen
(LOS)

127 Keith, GNSR bays end, looking to Inverness, July 1987 (RRFK)

128 Keith HR end, mainline on right and Portessie bay on left (LOS)

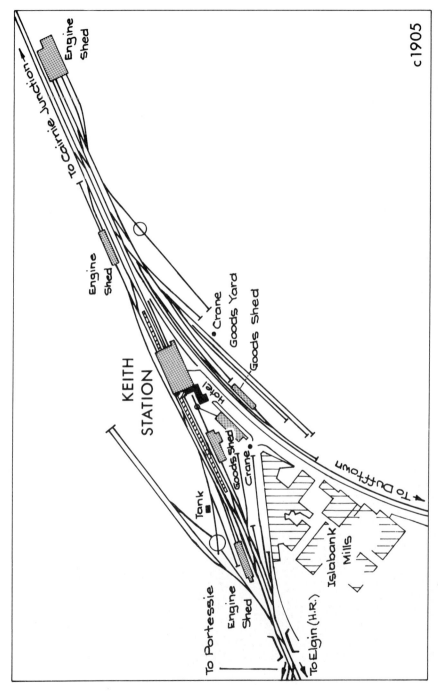

c1905

Map 30   Keith

already used for its local trains. In 1885 it was decided to install a bay platform for the branch line trains by converting the unused southern edge of the HR end of the through platform (128).

The station buildings were in the vee between the Inverness and Dufftown lines. There were HR and GNSR signal boxes and engine sheds at their respective ends of the station.

The station has been simplified with the terminal tracks between the HR and GNSR platforms having been removed. The old buildings were demolished in 1988 and a new station built on the site of the two GNSR bay platforms. The site of the Buckie bay is now in the new carpark.

Parts of Keith date from at least AD700 and it was nearby that the Jacobites fought their last successful action, defeating a section of the Duke of Cumberland's ('Stinking Billy' or 'Sweet William' depending upon your loyalties) army. Keith now comprises Old Keith, New Keith and Fife Keith. The new town was planned in 1750 by the Earl of Findlater who had already established lintmills in the district, hence Newmill. Fife Keith, across the Isla, was founded by the Earl of Fife in 1817.

The main industries are the manufacture of woollen goods and the distilling of whisky. Strathisla, the oldest working distillery in Scotland, is at Keith. G & G Kynoch's Isla Park Mills and the Strathisla distillery are open to the public and have guided tours, visitors' centres and shops. The two oldest places of interest are the Milton Tower (built in 1480 by the Ogilvies) which is in Station Road and the pack-horse bridge across the Isla, just off Regent Street. This bridge, built in 1609, which is the oldest in Morayshire and one of the oldest in Scotland connects Fife Keith and Keith. The names of its builders, Thomas Murray and Janet Lindsay, are carved in the south face.

The churches of Holy Trinity, St Rufus and St Thomas are all well worth a visit. St Thomas's Church is Roman Catholic and was built in 1830 with a façade which is a copy of Santa Maria de Angelis in Rome. 'The Incredulity of St Thomas' by François Dubois, is a part of the altar and was presented by Charles X of France who spent part of his exile in Scotland.

In August is held the Keith Fair. During the 1667 fair James Macpherson, the freebooter (see Banff, p 66, and Dufftown in *Speyside Railways*), was chased by Lord Braco. Macpherson tripped over a tombstone in the churchyard and was caught. Near Fife Keith churchyard is a pool, called the Gaun Pot, in which witches were drowned. Newmill was the birthplace in 1794 of James Gordon Bennett, the founder of the *New York Herald*. About 5½ miles outside the town is Eggs & Co, where egg decoration can be seen.

Facilities are available for golf, fishing, swimming, bowls and tennis. There are many good walks which can be undetaken from Keith. It has a comprehensive selection of shops, eating places, accommodation etc.

Leave the station and drive to the town centre. Turn right on to the A96. Just after the junction where the A95 leaves on the left the road crosses the mainline and the site of the junction was to the right. Chivas have destroyed the last part of the embankment to build bonded whisky storage. The embankment ends in an overbridge.

Aultmore (402534, OS sheet 28, Elgin)

Continue along the A96. Half a mile later is a turning to Haughs, where the line was in a cutting and Crooksmill siding, installed in 1911, was located (415513) and the line is readily visible from the roadside. Turn on to the B9016 and continue into Aultmore. Just after joining the B road the line is crossed. Turn left at Rowan Cottage by the HR gate and paling fencing.

The station here was originally known as Forgie but the name was changed and more sidings added from 1899 when the distillery was constructed and the community grew. Here there originally was a crossing loop with two platforms and a signal box at each end which lasted until 1907 when all signal boxes and signals were closed (129), probably at the same time the loop was converted to a siding (Map 31). The station building was the standard type for the line, as at Rathven.

The station master's house is still extant and to the west of it is the station site with the platforms, now covered in grass, still clearly discernible (130) with the edging stones in place. The site of the station building can be identified by the flat area on the eastern platform. The distillery now covers the site of the track to the north for some distance.

Leave on the B9013 heading north. Note the gates on the occupation crossing just north of the distillery. Some road improvements have destroyed the trackbed and the bridge at 401555 has been removed and the road straightened. The course of the railway, together with the abutments of dismantled bridges, can be discerned at intervals across the valley, although in parts it is ploughed out and in parts planted.

Enzie (410609, OS sheet 28, Elgin)

Continue along the B9013 until 398607 on to the unclassified road through Clochan village. At 406611 turn right up a track marked 'Enzie Station House and Cottage'. When the track forks, turn left. The gravel

129   Aultmore, looking to Portessie, 21 October 1954 (JLS)

130   Aultmore, looking north to Portessie, August 1988 (RRFK)

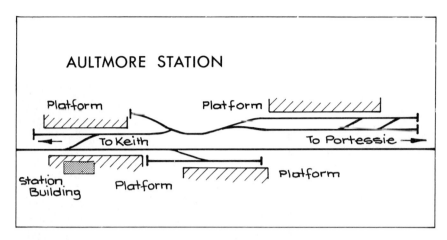

Map 31   Forgie/Aultmore

drive leads to the well maintained house and cottage, with attractive wooded grounds. This is a quiet and secluded site, well off the main road, and with luck a number of small animals, especially rabbits, moles and hedgehogs, may be observed.

The station had the standard station building with a crossing loop and two platforms with a signal box at either end but all of these, save the station building had disappeared by the general closure of the signal boxes on the branch which occurred in 1907. There were two sidings to the south of the station (131, Map 32).

The site of the platforms and goods dock are clearly visible although there is some undergrowth and the site of the track can be seen leaving the station (132). The station master's house (133) and the cottages (134) are in very good condition and still lived in. The former has magnificent views over the countryside all the way to the coast, Spey Bay and, on a clear day, the mountains across the Moray Firth.

Enzie is pronounced 'Ingy' and is believed to be a corruption of the Norman French 'L'Aunoy'. Return to the unclassified road and turn right.

Drybridge (435629, OS sheet 28, Elgin)

Follow the unclassified road in an easterly direction. At 420615 the remains of Cairnfield viaduct can sometimes be seen. The summer vegetation tends to hide this and a visit in the winter is recommended.

131 Enzie, looking south to Keith, *c* 1930 (CJF)

132 Enzie, August 1988 (RRFK)

133   Enzie stationmaster's house, August 1988 (RRFK)

134   Enzie station cottages, August 1988 (RRFK)

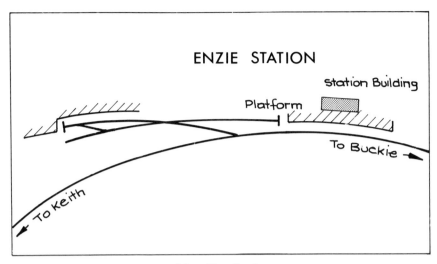

Map 32   Enzie

This, the largest viaduct on the line survived until the start of the Second World War when it was used for demolition practise by the Royal Engineers. It had four 30 feet spans, 76 feet above the burn it crossed. Other smaller bridges or the remains of demolished ones can be seen from the road along this section, e.g. at 418614 (intact) or 434625 (demolished). Just outside Drybridge village the road passes under one of the few remaining major structures on this line (435627). Pass through the village and turn right at 435630. The station is 100 yards on, just past a row of houses. The original road ran past those houses and over the line on a bridge, the abutments of which can still be seen to the left of the road. The road has been straightened and levelled. The single platform was to the right of where the road now crosses the trackbed.

This station was not one of the original stations but was authorised by the HR in 1885 without a loop. Unlike all the others it did not have a goods yard, probably because of the problems of finding sufficient level ground. However, when Buckie Town Council built a reservoir nearby a siding was provided about a quarter of a mile north of Drybridge station.

It consisted of a wooden platform and a very small wooden building, much smaller than the rest of those on this line (135). All has now gone (136) and the trackbed in both directions is very heavily overgrown, especially with gorse and other shrubs. It is however a haven for birds and butterflies, and the tiny wren was spotted near the station site. Just

135   Drybridge, looking south to Keith, *c* 1930 (CJF)

136   Drybridge, looking north to Portessie, showing abutments of old road
bridge, August 1988 (RRFK)

137   Letterfourie, looking south to Keith, *c* 1930 (CJF)

where the new road deviates from the old are a HR gate post and
gateposts which were the entry to the path to the platform.

The LMS renamed this Letterfourie (137) but it never operated under
that name.

Turn around and head north, there is a picnic site and viewpoint on
the unclassified road from Drybridge to Deskford.

Rathven (442646, OS sheet 28, Elgin)

At the A98 turn right and a mile further on pull into the layby on the left.
This is the old road which used to cross the line on a bridge. That has
been removed and the road levelled (138).

A path along the old station houses (139) leads to the trackbed at the
point where the sidings fanned out. From here to the north the line was
in a shallow cutting, although this has been filled in at one point to
provide farm access. This is an area of rolling pastureland supporting
mixed arable and livestock farming. The station was about a mile from
the village of Rathven. It had one platform with a standard HR building

138   Rathven, looking south (AJL)

139   Rathven station houses, August 1988 (RRFK)

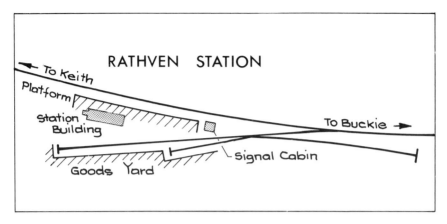

Map 33   Rathven

to the east of the line (140), a signal box at the northern end and, behind the station, a goods yard, entered from the Buckie direction, for the traffic to the Inchgower distillery (Map 33). From Rathven to Buckie cost 1*d*, in 1900, and took about 4 minutes, while to Keith it took 32 minutes and cost 11*d*. Allan Kennedy served as station master from the day the station opened to the day it closed.

140   Rathven (ML)

141   HR line south of Rathven, August 1988 (RRFK)

The station has gone completely, but the station houses have survived, albeit some of them somewhat modified. The site of the siding can be seen from the throat of the points, north of the station (138) and also from the layby. There are pleasant clumps of deciduous trees in the vicinity, and the hedgerows are full of rowan, wild roses, raspberries and brambles.

From the A98 a good view of the line curving away on an embankment to the south can be obtained including the demolished bridge (141).

The village of Rathven had a bede house for the refuge of lepers from 1226 and is known for its 'horse and cart cottage' and the Peter Fair. The first fair was held in 1686. The origin of its name is disputed, some claiming it is named after St Peter, the patron saint of Rathven Kirk while others believe it is called after a showman called Peter who was a regular visitor. Turn round and drive west along the A98.

Buckie (HR) (428656, OS sheet 28, Elgin)

Turn left on to the A942 to Buckie and turn right at Well Road. The line of the track can be observed here crossing the road. Turn left into Mill Crescent, which follows the curve of the railway. Turn left in to Hamilton Path, a cul de sac opposite Wallace Avenue. This also leads to the trackbed which appears as a grassy path between the houses.

This station was built on the west side of a slight curve and had the largest station building of any on the line. It was of the same basic structure as the others on the branch (e.g. Rathven), but had a transverse section at both ends instead of only one. The canopy only had four supports not the usual five and in place of a flat roof to the canopy the slope of the main building extended to cover it. The area under the canopy was thus enclosed on three sides instead of two and probably gave a little more shelter from the elements. There was a signal box at the southern end of the platform and a goods dock and three sidings to the north east, entered from the south (Map 34).

In places the track has been built over, but at the site of the station the platform outlines (filled in and tarmaced) with the base of the station building can be discerned. The station master's house is occupied and the goods shed and the loading dock are to be seen.

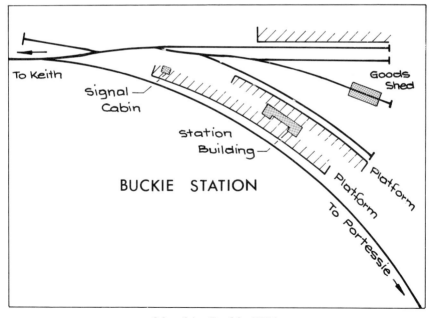

Map 34　Buckie (HR)

142   Buckie HR station in use as a golf clubhouse, 21 October 1954 (JLS)

After closure the station building was moved in 1939 to Portessie to become the Clubhouse of the Strathlene Golf Club (142), but in 1973 it was replaced.

Carry on along Mill Crescent and turn right in to Harbour Street, then right into Church Street. At the end of this turn right on to March Road, signposted to Rathven from where good views of the HR and GNSR lines to Portessie and the bridges over them can be obtained.

Return to the A942 and head east along the coast towards Portessie.

Portessie (447667, OS sheet 28, Elgin)

Continue along the A942 and at 445667 turn right and follow this road to the top of the hill. Portessie station is on the right, a little way along Station Road. See section III, p 100.

Endpiece—Doreen Betlem at Tillynaught Junction, asking the driver of the Banff branch train to stop at Bridgefoot, 1949 (PB)